# FROM HERE TO THERE

## Making Successful Transitions

ISI IGENEGBA

SCRIBES & SCROLLS

For information contact :

*Published by*
**SCRIBES & SCROLLS**
6A Jasper Ike Street, Off Hakeem Dickson Drive,
Lekki,Lagos.

*To contact the author:*
Email: isiigenegbabooks@gmail.com
Instagram: @isigenegba
Website: www.isibenedicta.com

Book and Cover Design by GLM Group

ISBN: 978-978-796-523-8

First Edition: March 2023

10 9 8 7 6 5 4 3 2 1

# IN THIS BOOK

**Author's Note**
**Introduction**
**Chap. 1: The Foundation of Transitions** 15

**Chap. 2: Why We Must Make Transitions** 43
*Classification of Transitions* 45
*Transition Rationalization* 51
**Chap. 3: The Big Picture** 61
*People In Your Life* 62
*The Places You Have Been* 67
*The Conditions You Have Experienced* 70

**Chap. 4: The Strategy of Hell** 75
*The Mephibosheth Syndrome* 83

**Chap. 5: The Reality Of Transitions** 89
*The Driver Of Transitions* 100
*The Call To Change* 111
*Change Of Perspective* 113
*The Burden Of Responsibility* 116
*The Place Of Encounters* 119
*Survival Vs Growth* 121

**Chap. 6: Reevaluating Your Transition** 125

**Chap. 7: Leveraging And Managing Relationships** 137
*Burden Bearers* 139
*The Reality* 154
*How To Manage Relationships In Transitions* 154
*Admissions* 169

**Chap. 8: My Blueprint for Making Successful Transitions** 175
*Acknowledge* 176
*Pray* 178
*Move* 182
*Repeat* 185

**Chap. 9: The Way forward** 189
*Three Tools for Successful Transitions* 194
*Afterword* 200

# *Author's Note*

# Author's Note

Hello,

I believe that you have picked up this book because your present season greatly resonates with the message of making successful transitions.

You could be in a season that is punctuated with a great big question mark, one riddled with confusion where you are neither able to define nor articulate what you are navigating.

On the other hand, you may very well be aware of what is going on but may be experiencing difficulty in accepting what it is. Regardless of which example suits you better, it is absolutely imperative to know that a delayed response will trip you into falling into the trap of the familiar where it becomes difficult to hear or see God's invitation to a new season. I am delighted that you are willing to commit to gaining the requisite knowledge to generate momentum for breaking into the many possibilities of this new season.

I have observed that God's modus operandi when He wants to reach us or reveal to us a new dimension in Him, is disruption. He swoops into our lives and divinely disrupts all that is familiar and has unconsciously become a stiffer of growth. You see, the unsuspecting enemy of God's next move in our lives is often the last experience or instruction we received from Him. We park ourselves right there, set up camp and echo the sentiments of Peter who desired to build tabernacles for Jesus, Elijah and Moses at the mountaintop.

These past or present experiences inevitably become cataracts on our spiritual eyes obscuring our ability to see what God is about to do next.

I have watched people go through life-altering situations that permanently marked and shaped them. I myself have had my fair share of such experiences. My plan, following marriage, like most women, was to have my children in quick succession so I could focus on raising them, but after having my first child, the script was not to be so. It took several years of fruitless trying and a series of miscarriages before my second child was finally born.

The journey to having my second child became a dramatic twist turning plot that I involuntarily featured as the main character. It was a season woven with intense warfare and struggle and the stories and lessons gleaned from that experience alone are worthy of an entire book. It went beyond your typical pregnancy and post-partum delivery scenario, the challenges in my case appeared to have been compounded.

Eventually, confusion and exhaustion caught up with me. My mind ran wild as I even contemplated leaving everything behind and starting a new life in Canada. Yes, I was that confused. In retrospect, I see how faithfully God has traveled with me. He transitioned me from confusion to someone who can help others define their seasons, give godly contexts to the events of their lives and empower them to respond accurately and access God's promise for their lives!

This book is more than personal development and educational material. It is God's wisdom simplified to help you out of your confusion and lead you to what God has promised you. As you will discover, I did not share these strategies to satisfy an itch to write a book. I truly desire to see that you are blessed by what you are about to learn, and my prayer is that, as you open your heart to receive and consciously apply them, you will find peace and direction to move from where you are to where you ought to be. Granted, it won't be an overnight miracle, but your continuous dedication to employing the lessons from this book will bring you closer to God's plan.

Whether you're struggling with your marriage or relationships, struggling with your career or business, or wondering what God wants you to do next, this book provides valuable guidelines on how you can find the answers to your needs.

I look forward to hearing and sharing testimonies of how your life changed from applying the lessons you are about to learn, and I pray for the grace and wisdom for you to go through this phase successfully and come into the fullness of God's will for your life.

Thank you for betting on yourself. From here, it can only get better.

God bless you.
*Apostle Isi Igenegba*

# *Introduction*

# *Introduction*

During a meeting in 2020, God told me that there are people who He has called and anointed to do great things, but they are held back by pain, shame, anxiety, fear, and procrastination. Despite God's wonderful plans for them, they are stuck in cycles of pain and confusion.

As He spoke to me, He gave me a distinctive word; "Show them how to successfully transition from where they have been and where they are to where I have sent them." This is the revelation that led me to pen this book. Compared to other projects I have done, this book stems from deep personal experience. When I started writing it, I was flooded with memories of various experiences and emotions that I had not fully come to terms with. In hindsight, I realize I could have handled a few of those situations differently. For most of us, our vulnerability to transition tends to get us embroiled in our emotions, making it easy to miss out on the blessings of the season and instead be rendered seemingly helpless to the plans of our enemies. I have been through multiple seasons over the years; some seasons unfolded as open-and-shut cases of clarity and pursuit while others are best described as a merry-go-round of paralysis.

In 2015, I had a reason to leave the ministry where I was serving as a Pastor. It was overwhelming because the ministry was everything I knew and had; my friends, family, mentors, mentees, and even my job was in the ministry. During that season, my life seemed to fall apart and the lights went out. It was a baffling experience that I struggled to make sense of and that led me to venture into several things. I started a business, attended John C. Maxwell Certification Program, and did other things in an attempt to escape the effects of what happened. Through these experiences, and as God used them as tools in my journey, God has given me guidelines to help people recognize and successfully maximize the blessings of transitions. That's exactly what you get from this book.

If everything has always been bright and beautiful for you, don't get carried away. Transitions come to everyone and all you can do is prepare. Transitions are often frightening and confusing experiences, but the ability to understand them and express those experiences is empowering for the next phase of your life.

This book reevaluates the role your background and mindsets have played in determining how much you have achieved, and with this, you will be able to better piece the puzzles of your life together and realize how various junctions of life eventually intersected for you to arrive at this point. You will also learn how to unbiasedly recognize and define seasons for what they are, and not what your emotions try to make out of them. I have also included some key questions that you need to answer to gain clarity and strength to successfully navigate the transition. The correct answer often depends on your ability to ask the right question.

As a minister, I understand how much impact the past has on the possibilities of the future. As a result, you will learn how to manage the present and future seasons of your life, from this book. It will empower you with spiritual knowledge and strategies to confront and recover the blessings from transitions you didn't recognize or maximize in the past. It is an illusion to assume that I'm perfect and always go through transitions unscathed, but the only advantage I have is that I have been given a divine strategy to handle it.

These are the important strategies I have shared with you in this book. As transitions are continuous, I pray that the blessings of this book will empower you with wisdom to make the most of every season you experience. Amen.

*Apostle Isi Igenegba*

## *Chapter 1*

# THE FOUNDATION OF TRANSITIONS

*When you become too self-sufficient, you may fail to recognize the need for growth and change, and may even resist the very transitions that God is leading you towards.*

## *Chapter 1*

# THE FOUNDATION OF TRANSITIONS

Seasons of what we deem as progress and success can lead us to become complacent and comfortable with the prevailing status quo. This can be attributed to several reasons. For example, we may start to rely too heavily on our own abilities or resources, rather than seeking God's guidance and provision. In other words, our strength can easily become a god or we may use the faulty standards of the world as a yardstick to measure success and progress instead of the plans and purposes God has outlined for our lives.

The danger in becoming too comfortable in your current circumstances is that you may miss the opportunities that God is providing for you to grow and step into new areas of calling and ministry. This is especially true when you face challenges or setbacks that require you to lean more fully on God's strength and wisdom.

> *"When you become too self-sufficient, you may fail to recognize the need for growth and change"*

When you become too self-sufficient, you may fail to recognize the need for growth and change, and may even resist the very transitions that God is leading you toward.

This posture engenders difficulty in discerning when God is leading you beyond your current circumstances. Joseph in the Bible undergoes various transitions as God stretches him out in his purpose and the unique role he played in God's redemption plan for the nation of Israel.

At one point, he was under authority and then at another ***in*** authority and even at other times, in authority *w*hile still under authority. We initially meet him as a beloved son who becomes a beloved slave rising to the ranks of house manager then he becomes a beloved chief prisoner and then finally a beloved prime minister. From the pit to the prison to the palace, Joseph remained committed to God and used his skills, gifts and graces to serve others.

> *"God's seeming lateness or "absence" is His way of re-engineering all things for your good"*

And so must we. Where you aren't affected by the status quo of previous seasons, you may also find yourself emotionally attached to the challenging seasons in your life, clinging to them despite the setbacks and pain they bring. Yet if you embrace God's sovereignty and wisdom, you can begin to see these seasons as opportunities for pruning and preparation, shaping you for the destiny that lies ahead.

There are a few reasons you might become emotionally attached to challenging seasons in your life.

One reason is that these seasons may become familiar to you, even if they are difficult. You may develop habits and coping mechanisms that help you navigate these challenges, and you may feel a sense of security in the familiarity of your circumstances, even if they are painful.

Another reason is that you may derive a sense of identity or purpose from these challenges. For example, you may feel that your struggles give you a unique perspective or testimony that can be used to help others. Or you may feel that your hardships are necessary for you to grow and mature spiritually.

While there may be some truths to these perspectives, it is important to recognize that God doesn't want you to remain in a state of perpetual struggle or pain. His desire is for you to experience abundant life and to fulfill the calling He has placed on your life.

When you cling to challenging seasons, you may also be resisting the transitions that God is leading you toward. You may be afraid or weary of the unknown or uncertain about your ability to succeed in new circumstances. You may also be 'tabernacle' in past hurts or failures that make it difficult for you to trust God's plans for your future.

> "*Your life is a part of a greater story that God is telling from Heaven*

To overcome this attachment to challenging seasons, you must first acknowledge the sovereignty of God and be in agreement with the truth that He really is in control of all and that He has a plan for your life that is good and pleasing to Him. You must also recognize that your struggles are not the defining feature of your identity, but rather opportunities for growth and transformation.

By surrendering your fears and insecurities to God and trusting in His provision and guidance, you can move forward with confidence and faith, knowing that He is with you every step of the way.

As such, irrespective of how dark or bleak the conditions present themselves, you are to understand that God's seeming lateness or "absence" is His way of re-engineering all things for your good.

Such seasons are often first introduced with a lot of incertitude and puzzlement. Nonetheless, the overarching mindset that should govern you in such times is to consider it all an opportunity for growth and transformation. Embracing this mindset is what separates those who end up being bound by demonic burdens of hopelessness and anxiety from those who find the joy of knowing they're aligned with Heaven's agenda for their time.

> *"You can't just coast along and expect everything to fall into place"*

As you navigate life, it is important to maintain a deep understanding that everything that happens to you is not merely a coincidence. As a believer, your life is part of a greater story that God is telling from Heaven, and every season that you encounter has a purpose in God's overall plan for your life. However, the enemy also has a plan to see you fall short of God's purpose for your life, so it is crucial to remain discerning and stay aligned with God's script for your life.

The enemy invests a great deal of effort into trying to create chaos and destruction in your life during certain seasons, but it is important to remember that God always has His own plan and desire for you. He has a system in place to equip and empower you to overcome any obstacle or challenge that come your way so that you can fulfill His purposes and bring about His desired outcome.

Ultimately, every season you. Experience is an opportunity for you to grow and learn, and become more equipped to fulfill your God-given purpose

> "*You need to make decisions that are critical to the advancement of heaven's agenda*

By maintaining your focus on God and staying in tune with His will for your life, you can overcome any obstacle that the enemy may throw your way, and ultimately achieve the fullness of what God has planned for you.

What we are doing in this book is positioning and bringing you into all that the Lord has pre-programmed and designated for you to enter into in this season of your life.

The reality is that, even though time keeps moving forward and you enter into a new season, you may not feel ready or equipped to handle the changes that come with it. For example, you may start a new job or move to a new city but still feel like you're stuck in your old habits and ways of thinking.

This can be especially true when it comes to your purpose and power - that is, your sense of direction and ability to make things happen. It is possible to feel like you're in a new season, but still lack the confidence or clarity you need to truly thrive in it.

This is why it is so important to take deliberate steps to steward each season of your life well. You need to actively seek out the resources and guidance you need to succeed, and be willing to put in the work to align yourself with God's plan for your life. You can't just coast along and expect everything to fall into place- you need to be intentional about your growth and development.

> *"Experience from previous seasons is not always sufficient to navigate a new one"*

By doing this, you can gradually start to feel more in tune with the new season and the opportunities it presents. You can start to tap into your sense of purpose and power and use them to make a positive impact in the world around you. But it all starts with recognizing that just because the calendar has turned, it doesn't necessarily mean you're fully equipped to handle what's coming next.

To do this, you need to go beyond simply making good decisions for yourself and your family. You need to make decisions that are critical to the advancement of heaven's agenda.

This means seeking God's will for your life and being intentional about aligning yourself with His purposes. It means being willing to step out of your comfort zones and take risks, knowing that God will be with you every step of the way.

Ultimately, stewarding a new season well, requires a deep level of commitment and dedication. It means being willing to put in the work to ensure that every part of your life is aligned with God's plan for you. However, when you do this, you can be confident that you'll be equipped with everything you need to fulfill your destiny and bring glory to God in the process.

**AVOID MAKING THIS MISTAKE**

In embarking on a new season, it is important to let go of any preconceived expectation and yield oneself to the encounters that will enable the fulfillment of God's preordained plans.

Experiences from previous seasons are not always sufficient to navigate a new one. This is where one's willingness to partner with heaven is critical. When you get used to doing things a certain way, it can be difficult to do it differently.

> *"The realities of the transition prepare and empower you for what is coming"*

However, one of the dangers in being accustomed to tradition, whether it leads you to the fullness of God's plan for your life or not, is the risk of not promptly yielding to the silent changes that might be going on, particularly if you have been used to a measure of progress and success. This can lead to missed opportunities for growth and development, as well as missed opportunities to fulfill your destiny and purpose.

In difficult seasons, it is easier to stay committed to hearing God's instructions and have a heart ready to move as He commands. However, when things are going well, it is easy to assume that one is in alignment with God's will for the season. Therefore, having a heart fixed on understanding God's will every season and deploying all available resources to fulfill it is crucial.

As God orchestrates various conditions to serve His purpose in one's life, the outcome of these conditions depends on how they are interpreted and responded to.

A season that is meant to prepare one for new levels of intimacy and service could end up making one weary, discouraged, or bitter if not approached with the right attitude because it is not by power nor by might; it is by the spirit of the Living God.

*Matthew 4:1-3;*

*"Then Jesus was led by the Spirit into the wilderness to be tempted[a] by the devil. After fasting for forty days and forty nights, he was hungry. The tempter came to him and said, 'If you are the Son of God, tell these stones to become bread.'"*

Think about it. Jesus; God incarnate, was led to the wilderness by the Holy Spirit in His full glory, to begin a new season of His life. He yielded Himself to consecration, and afterward, the next encounter He had wasn't with a 'Host of Angels' or the 'Seven Spirits of God'. It wasn't even a platform to showcase Him to the world.

> *"As you step into this season, you are responsible for what you make out of your experience"*

Just at the prime of a new season, what greets Him is something that threatens the realization of what the season carried. You must understand something; just because you have entered into a new season does not mean you have overcome all trials.

The experiences you go through, during transitions, prepare and empower you for what is coming. You must build the capacity to handle what is coming. The Temptations that will come after you step into a new season, and the way you handle and maneuver through them, will determine the power you will walk in for the rest of the season and your life in general.

> *"What you get from Him depends on how much you are willing to engage."*

Sometimes, while you are still trying to understand why you had to leave your previous season, the enemy is going to begin to push certain adversities in front of you, in an attempt to weaken and paralyze you. They will stop at no length in ensuring that you are unable to galvanize yourself to do what God has called you to do.

This isn't the time to jump on trends or share your experiences on social media. You need to go on a retreat, asking the Holy Spirit to empower and saturate you to the point where He can regulate your desires —your thirst and your hunger.

As you step into this season, you are responsible for what you make out of your experience.

Yes, God has a plan for you. He has all it takes to bring you into that plan, no doubt. He even trusts that you will be sensitive enough to align yourself with His plan. But the inescapable truth is that what you get from Him depends on how much you are willing to engage. What you come for is what you get, regardless of what He has to offer.

*John 7:37-39:*

*"In the last day, that great day of the feast, Jesus stood and cried, saying, if any man thirst, let him come unto me, and drink. He that believeth on me, as the scripture hath said, out of his belly shall flow rivers of living water. (But this spake he of the Spirit, which they that believe on him should receive: for the Holy Ghost was not yet given; because that Jesus was not yet glorified.)"*

First of all, Jesus says *"If any man thirsts, let him come unto me and drink."* That means some people come to Jesus just because He affirms them. You might be reading this book just because you are thirsty, not because you truly believe.

You approach Jesus, just because you need clarity on what you are going through, and your engagement with Him is always along the lines of, "Oh God, I want to get it right", "God, hey, I want my family to be better", " Oh God, I want my spouse to be more supportive." "Lord, we need more money for the business," "Ah, this year, I'm believing and trusting you to give me this or that."

> *"You will not only be awakened, but you become the river of awakening for a generation"*

There are two dimensions of operation when it comes to the way we engage Christ. Some people come just because of their thirst, and Jesus says whoever comes because he's thirsty, I will give him water to drink. Because I'm a Good Master and a kind God, people cannot come to me in need of bread and I will give them stone; they cannot come to me in need of fish and I will give them scorpion.

For those that come because they just need to quench their thirst, their heart posture is the same.

*"I don't care who you are. I don't care what you can do. I'm not interested in engaging in your sanctification or circumcision. I'm just coming because I'm thirsty."*

When you come, He will give you what you are crying out for. Nevertheless, there is another set of people who are not just saying, "God, meet my thirst." He says, among the people that come, he that believes in me, out of his belly shall flow rivers of Living Water.

Some will come to Jesus in this season because they want to drink. You come because you want a spiritual awakening. They want answers to their numerous questions and an assurance that their expectations are not going to be cut short. You will receive the awakening and the validations you seek, which will only last for a while, but others who engage the Spirit and they become Rivers. If you are in this dimension, you will not only be awakened, but you become the river of awakening for a generation.

> *"Accept the responsibility to partner with the Spirit to become the momentum of this generation and your niche."*

The two dimensions of engaging Christ in this season are I.) The dimension of thirst and hunger and ii.) The dimension of expression, creation, and restoration.

He says, "Out of their belly will flow rivers of Living Water," and we know what the Bible spoke about concerning this water. Everywhere the water went, it healed the land and the people and brought about restoration.

You have the power to decide whether your engagement with God will stop at God merely responding to your personal requests or it will extend further to receive supernatural capacity and become God's restorative tool in the world. It is entirely up to you.

> *"They empower the Ecclesia to manifest the wisdom and power of God wherever they are found."*

This emphasis is critical because we are setting the pace for the remaining part of the book and for how you respond to your current season. You need to decide who you want to be by reading this book because when God begins to unveil His plan for the season, I pray you will neither be a spectator, nor the flustered character trying to play catch up or worse still, a Sanballat or Tobias casting aspersions on those who are fully maximizing their season.

One of the things I consistently admonish my team about is the necessity of recognizing when a shift has taken place within me and when I am about to make a move.

I tell them not to imagine in their hearts that the Apostle Isi they knew yesterday is the same Apostle Isi with them the next day because, overnight, it is possible for me to make a major spiritual journey to a new place in surrender, triggered by revelation and genuine repentance. The said spiritual journey could perhaps be the equivalent of two years as measured by our side of eternity. As a result, in a space of a few hours in prayer, my thinking and faith could have experienced an entirely new paradigm shift which will be reflected in my speech and actions. That is why it will be erroneous to attempt to take me back to a mindset from about four years ago.

Spiritual journeys are about receiving revelation and your willingness to trust the Lord to carry you from point A to point B. It has nothing to do with physical time. Some people have lived for a hundred years but, in the realm of the spirit, they only lived for 10 years because they stretched the journey of spiritual 10 years across a hundred years. Also, some have lived for 30 years but in the spirit realm, they have lived almost 90 years, because they used every day of their lives to make profound moves with and for God.

> "*Every time you rise in your level of mastery, you rise in authority.*"

Like David says in Psalms 90:12;

*"Teach us to number our days, that we may apply our hearts to wisdom."*

The wisdom of God is beyond knowing good things or being able to give sound advice on issues. David was saying Wisdom comes alongside the man that is able to understand that every day is an opportunity to initiate and execute divine partnership. Your ability to steward your days and your seasons effectively is what attracts the army and resources of wisdom to you. The reason certain kinds of people can partner with your life and destiny is that you are still ordering your days very carefully.

Decide not to be a spectator in this season. You don't have to be the one that watches others ride upon the wings of the spirit in what God is set to do in your space. Accept the responsibility to partner with the Spirit to become the momentum of this generation and your niche. You can be the one that generates spiritual energy everywhere you go, carrying the revival fire, power, and wisdom of God.

> “*Don't plateau around the Success of your previous Season so much that you are too relaxed to move at God's* ______

When you decide to take things into your hands and explore the fullness of God for your current season, it creates a significant impact on people because for you to reposition and respond to life, it changes how you interpret and navigate life.

When you go through such a change of state, it can alter the way you handle situations, make decisions, and view the world around us. This can be both exciting and challenging, as you adapt to new circumstances and roles.

Notwithstanding, the risk of this change is such that, regardless of the outcome of your transition, the change you experience redefines your life going forward. As a result of this risk, it becomes imperative to be diligent in your pursuit of the accurate posture and response to the experience(s) you are going through, to guide and help you preserve the integrity of God's plan for your life.

## MANAGING SEASONS ACCURATELY

As you go through different seasons, you become more grounded; you gain a deeper understanding of who you are and what you want, you redefine the way you perceive the world around you, and you get a sense of stability and direction that can help you align better with God's agenda for your life.

> *"To seek out new resources and support to help you adapt"*

As you would have realized, the purpose of what God is doing in and through you is to bring you into the uniqueness of our calling and ordination. Even though we all have a heritage in Christ, you must understand that the mantle upon your life speaks about your peculiar spiritual covering. The results of your accurate, diligent engagement with Christ and His systems will bring you into a unique reality, different from what others would come into, even if they followed the same path. The mantle of your life designates and empowers you in your unique assignments.

The unique longings of your heart, your quest for more, and your gifts and talents are pointers to the unique office God has called you into. As you step into new seasons, you are being prepared for the levels of promotion that your office requires. Every attempt to make things work by your own strength and wisdom will prove futile because it is the office you operate that compels men, systems, and the Heavens to collaborate with you.

In the limitation of your wisdom, you might not understand the full scope of your office, not to mention the tools, resources, and strategies that would ensure your efficiency, effectiveness, and excellence, but if you yield yourself to the protocols of the office you occupy, the office has, in itself, the grace to attract all that makes for the manifestation of its glory.

Your office makes you devoted to God from whom you received the mantle, to ensure that you can know His intention per time and align appropriately.

Although your office is eternal and spiritual, by the level of government and priesthood you have been called to represent, it is also your physical covering and contains your unique Ministry attributes.

*Ephesians 4:8-13*

*"This is why it says: 'When he ascended on high, he took many captives and gave gifts to his people.' (What does 'he ascended' mean except that he also descended to the lower, earthly regions? He who descended is the very one who ascended higher than all the heavens, to fill the whole universe.) So Christ himself gave the apostles, the prophets, the evangelists, the pastors, and teachers, to equip his people for works of service, so that the body of Christ may be built up, until we all reach unity in the faith and in the knowledge of the Son of God and become mature, attaining to the whole measure of the fullness of Christ."*

> *"Be patient with yourself and to allow yourself the time and space you need to adapt to the new circumstances."*

Many times, you hear these things and you think about them in light of what we now know the Church to be, but that's not what Jesus gave. The Gifts He gave were designated offices that, in themselves, have all they require to function maximally and fulfill your purpose.

Think about a typical office e.g., being the Minister of Foreign Affairs in any nation. Regardless of who the Minister is, so long as they have taken the oath of office, they have access to everything the office requires. The office is beyond a title. It possesses and is entitled to all it needs to be effective, from human resources, budgetary allocation, authority to make decisions and enact them, the necessary partnerships that facilitate their operations, a seat at the table to negotiate better agreements on issues concerning their sphere of influence and all that.

> “*Your attitude to the seasons of your life prepares you to either inherit or forfeit the Promise of God.*”

When you hear about the operations of Apostles, Prophets, Pastors, Teachers and Evangelists, God was not talking about a church building or Sunday service as we have become accustomed to. He was talking about spiritual allocations and positioning that make power available to men in the realm of the spirit. He was talking about the level of access men have to earthly and heavenly resources, in terms of the collaborations they have with the Angelic host, the doors that you have the power to open in the realm of the spirit and the systems you have been called to steward on the earth.

The relevance of these offices goes beyond the typical church operations; they empower the Ecclesia to manifest the wisdom and power of God wherever they are found.

The grace of a teacher gives you the ability to receive Heavenly information and strategies, distill them into actionable bits and concisely release it to your generation.

The Pastoral Dimension gives you the anointing in the Spirit realm to galvanize people and lead your organization in such a way that people would want to work with you consistently.

The Apostolic gives you the capacity to break ground in your sphere of influence, to develop new models, processes and systems that transform and reposition industry patterns and reset the standards.

> *"By delaying or resisting transition, you may be delaying or resisting the fulfillment of your vision and purpose"*

Could it be that the current season of your life is related to how you have handled your office in the past? You might have either rejected, neglected or deviated from your calling, for whatever reason, and heaven wants to reposition and realign you. You must understand that your response to your calling is what determines how far you go with God.

You can either choose the path of convenience and build a career that will come short of God's plan for you, or you yield yourself to the protocol of mastery, so much so that you become one who can represent the Kingdom. Every time you rise in your level of mastery, you rise in authority.

During seasons of transitions, God supernaturally appoints people and thrust them into positions that they never imagined were possible. In such seasons of favor and responsibility, what makes you exercise authority effectively is your level of mastery of the government of God over your life and calling.

Adam and Eve were blessed with dominion and authority, but they did not understand government. They needed to qualify for mastery by passing the tests. It is the government that qualifies you to walk in the power that you have been given.

The same thing happened with Jesus in the wilderness. The purpose of His temptation was to test His level of mastery. By passing the test, He showed that He could bear the weight of God's government, and, by such mastery, He had the authority to release power.

Overwhelming seasons, like the one you might be experiencing, are an attempt to test your level of mastery, to prepare you to represent God accurately. Mastery empowers you, such that, not only will Satan not be able to toy with you, but he will also not use you as a pawn in his game.

> *"By assuming responsibility for your mistakes or failures, your children may have less time and energy to focus on their own goals and pursuits"*

As you grow in mastery and become yielded to the realities of your office, God begins to use you as the one who tells His story on earth. Imagine having to spend your life doing all you consider as faithful service to God, only to get to Heaven and realize that you were telling a story that heaven did not recognize. You might be commended for making it to Heaven, but you are likely to miss the reward of alignment.

In pursuit of mastery, as you go through certain seasons, you will find yourself developing a different view on issues. The fullness of what God is bringing you into is such that you will be governed by a different set of rules that enhance your operation, and you must be intentional about how you handle opinions that no longer serve what God is doing.

These changes in perspective can also affect the way you respond to life's challenges and opportunities. As you adapt to your new circumstances, you may find yourself approaching problems and situations in new ways and developing new coping mechanisms and strategies for dealing with change.

The promises of navigating difficult seasons successfully might occupy your mind and make you assume that those around you should appreciate what you are going through and possibly contribute to it.

The reality is that the experiences you go through will be misinterpreted by others who may not understand the changes. Your obedience can also create a positive and supportive environment for your children challenges and opportunities you are going through or how they are affecting you.

> “Your obedience can also create a positive and supportive environment for your children”

It is important to remember that everyone experiences change differently, and it is okay to take all the time you need to adjust to your new circumstances. This can be especially true if the transition you are experiencing is significant or transformative, as it may be difficult for others to relate to or comprehend it.

Knowing that people are likely to misinterpret or be unable to contribute to your experiences, it is also important to learn how to communicate your needs and feelings to others. By being open and honest about your own experiences and needs, you can help others to better understand and support you as you move through different phases of your life.

When going through these seasons of change, it can be helpful to identify the changes you are experiencing and how they are impacting you. This can help you to better understand your own needs and feelings and to communicate them to others.

It is important to be open and receptive to learning new things during transitions, even if it feels uncomfortable or unfamiliar. This may require you to step outside your comfort zone and try new things, or to seek out new resources and support to help you adapt.

Learning new habits, attitudes, and perspectives can also be an exciting and rewarding experience, as it allows you to grow and evolve as you move through different phases of your life.

By embracing change and stepping outside your comfort zone, you can discover new strengths and passions, and develop a greater sense of purpose and direction.

This process can bring out the best version of you, as you adapt and grow in response to new challenges and opportunities.

It is important to remember, however, that transitions can be painful and challenging, and that it is normal to feel overwhelmed or uncertain at times. It is also important to be patient and allow yourself the time and space you need to adapt to the new circumstances.

Sometimes, transitions can be incomplete or truncated, leaving you feeling stuck or uncertain about your direction. However, your attitude to the seasons of your life prepares you to either inherit or forfeit the promise of God.

As with many others, there is the possibility of making a name for yourself because of the sacrifices you have made in the past. You plateau around the success of your previous season so much that you are too relaxed to move at God's command. Your commitment should be such that, irrespective of the pains that you may be experiencing, you will remain focused on the bigger picture and your long-term goals.

This is not the time to count your steps or seek validation from people. It requires a rapid response time, as you may not have the leisure time to fully process or prepare for the changes you are experiencing. It is essential to be flexible and adaptable and to be open to new opportunities and challenges as they arise.

Not yielding accurately and completely to the seasons of your life can have significant consequences, both for you and those around you.

Two potential consequences of how you respond to seasons of transition include; (i) Choosing to delay obedience. This could result in someone else fulfilling the vision and receiving the promise, and your disobedience will become an inherited burden on your children. (ii) Choosing to yield diligently to what God wants to achieve through you. When you do this, your obedience will then become the stable foundation for your children to relate with God on other weightier matters.

When you respond to your seasons of transitions, here are three possible consequences or the results of your obedience or disobedience;

### -SOMEONE ELSE FULFILLING THE VISION AND RECEIVING THE PROMISE

You must understand that you are not the only one with the vision. In the spirit of preservation, God puts similar ideas in the hearts of various people in a specific location, generation or type, and the fulfillment of that idea is tied to such people.

When you are reluctant to act on instructions as you receive them, there is a possibility that someone from your region rises to do the very things that were asked of you, in the same way you were asked to do it, only for you to end up feeling frustrated and disappointed.

This can be especially frustrating and disappointing if you believe that you have been called by God to a particular purpose or mission, and if you feel that you have been delayed or hindered in some way.

For example, if you have been called to a particular job or career, but fail to respond to the opportunity that would take you there, you may miss out on fulfilling your calling. Instead, someone else may step into the role and receive the blessings and rewards that were meant for you.

It is important to recognize that this consequence is not a punishment or a sign of God's disfavor, but rather a natural result of your own choices and actions. By delaying or resisting transition, you may be delaying or resisting the fulfillment of your vision and purpose.

To avoid this consequence, it is important to yield accurately and completely to seasons of transitions and to be obedient to the guidance and direction of God. By doing so, you can ensure that you are in the right place at the right time to fulfill your calling and receive the blessings and rewards that are meant for you.

## -YOUR DISOBEDIENCE BECOMES A BURDEN ON YOUR CHILDREN

If you fail to yield accurately to the seasons of your life, there is a possibility that your children may feel obligated to correct your mistakes or to assume responsibility for your failures. This leaves them with little or no time to discover their calling and purpose.

For example, if you have been called to fulfill an assignment, but fail to yield to the transition that would take you there, your children may feel the need to step in and fill the gap. They may feel pressured to succeed where you have failed or to fulfill the vision and purpose that you have abandoned. This can be a heavy burden for your children to bear, as they may feel as though they have to choose between their dreams and your expectations.

In addition to the emotional and psychological toll that this burden can take on your children, it can also have practical consequences.

## -YOUR OBEDIENCE BECOMES THE STABLE FOUNDATION FOR YOUR CHILDREN

By setting a good example and showing them how to navigate change and uncertainty, you can help them to develop the skills and resilience they need to thrive in their own lives.

Your obedience can also create a positive and supportive environment for your children, as they work to discover their calling and purpose.

For example, if you are obedient to the guidance and direction of God in your life, your children may be more likely to seek out and follow their path. They may be more confident in their abilities and more open to new experiences and challenges. They are also more likely to develop their sense of purpose and direction, as they see the positive results of obedience in your life.

By following your calling and purpose, you can create a sense of stability and security for your children, and help them to feel more grounded and confident as they navigate their transitions.

Chapter 2

# WHY WE MUST MAKE TRANSITIONS

*The reality is not about what you want, but what you have become as a result of your experiences.*

## Chapter 2

# WHY WE MUST MAKE TRANSITIONS

In all our endeavors, our goal is to improve on our current level of growth with the hope of coming to the fullness of what God has purposed for us. Oftentimes, notwithstanding the validity of your desire for more, you might get too used to a certain experience that threatens the realization of the next phase of your life. The reality is not about what you want, but what you have become as a result of your experiences. There is a tendency for you to identify yourself with your current level, whether it is be pleasant or painful, so much that you shy away from the call of God to step up to a new season.

This was the issue with Joshua. He was used to following and trusting the leadership of Moses. Whether they were up the mountain or there was a need to visit an enemy's territory to gather intelligence, Joshua was comfortable with taking instructions from Moses.

> *"The reality is not about what you want, but what you have become as a result of your experiences"*

After all, who wouldn't submit to the only person God was communicating with directly? In following Moses, there were times when they both went up the mountain together, to get messages from God, but when God took Moses to show him the Promised Land, Joshua wasn't there.

Although Joshua was not privy to the details of his Master's death, it was natural for the people of Israel to turn to him for direction, as they would have done with Moses.

There he was, staying true to the training he had received from Moses. His style was still based on what the Lord had told Moses, but if Israel would make any significant progress, there needed to arise a leader who could receive instructions from God as Moses did, and lead the people to the will of God.

Have you ever wondered why God still appeared to Joshua to give him a definite assignment to fulfill, even when it was evident that the people were listening to him after Moses' death?

Everyone body in Israel, including Joshua, was bound by the instructions of God as given by Moses. They moved as Moses instructed, but after Moses' death, they had to stick with the instructions that governed their daily lives.

There wasn't any mention of progress regarding their journey to Canaan, although they kept the instructions.

> *"God's plan for Israel wasn't just to have them live by a set of rules, but to bring them into a place he had promised"*

God's plan for Israel wasn't just to have them live by a set of rules, but to bring them into a place He had promised Abraham. From being a follower, He had to call Joshua into the office of one who can lead the people into God's plan for them.

This is the reality of transitions; God calls you out of what you are used to, regardless of how much success you have achieved, and brings you into a position where you can faithfully steward.

It is a process of transforming your experiences into tools for the advancement of God's plan, where followers rise to their authoritative positions in Christ to influence systems for the Kingdom. Transitions are an attempt to refine and position you to maximize the fullness of the next season of your life. There has to be a corresponding change of nature that realigns you with provisions for the new season.

> *"Transitions are an attempt to refine and position you to maximize the fullness of the next season of your life"*

Despite the glorious potential of a transition to bring you to the next level of God's agenda, it matters how you respond to the call. Your ability to accurately discern the seasons – people, times, instructions, and places of your life and respond by yielding to God's plan is what ensures that you partake in the blessings of transitions.

## CLASSIFICATION OF TRANSITIONS

Transitions are classified into about three different categories, thus;

### 1. SILENT TRANSITIONS:

Every now and then in life, you will come across what I term "mild shake-ups." While these experiences are not necessarily earth-shattering in nature, they are defining enough to leave a measurable impression and effect on you. God uses them to prime you and your environment for what He is set to do.

Those are the times when you suddenly get a persistent nudge to pray and you find yourself waking up at night, but you don't seem to understand what is happening. It could be times when you feel a need to change how you dress or just how you relate with some people. Regular things like this, although supposedly innocuous, could be God's way of bringing you into what He has prepared for you in the new season.

There's barely ever anything obvious or dramatic about this type of transition; it doesn't call for a relocation or the end of a relationship. It can be accommodated by your current framework, although the goal is to refine the framework for the next move of God.

> *"Your ability to be sensitive to those simple, silent nudging in your heart and to steward them diligently"*

The mildness of this transition makes it so that you would rarely ever think it could be the reason for the newness you experience in the next season, but it is.

Your adeptness in being sensitive and cognizant of those silent and simple nudges and responding appropriately to them would define everything else.

**2. OBVIOUS TRANSITIONS:**

Sometimes, transitions can start silently but progress to become obvious, even to the people around you. During obvious transitions, the goal is to weed out people, systems, structures, and patterns that don't serve where God is taking you. It is not business as usual. Whereas in silent transitions, God is trying to refine you but in obvious transitions, He wants to define the systems around you.

He will give you instructions on what to change and things to act on. The impact and relevance of such instructions might affect your current system, although it won't require an overhaul. For example, you might have agreed to start something-a job, go back to school, a business, or whatever and you had things you had hoped to achieve upon starting and going through the journey.

> *"During obvious transitions, the goal is to weed out people, systems, structures, and patterns that*

When all you agreed to achieve during the project or after you might have concluded with it, as the case may be, regardless of how productive you were in that season, it would be unproductive to remain in that season when God is calling you to do something new.

Regardless of your success in the previous season, you know why you had to go through it, and it is expected that you recognize the need to transition afterward.

The result of this transition will surely affect what you are used to, but it is easier to handle because it is powered by the fulfilment of an agreement, hence you are going into the new season with the strength and support of people. Such transitions come on the heels of the need to grow and evolve, and your ability to handle them with that perspective would bring you into the new season ready to flourish.

**3. TURBULENT TRANSITIONS:**

Unlike the first two, this type results in a total overhauling of what you are used to.

An example would be a case where God asks you to leave a place without explaining to either you or those you were with. The disillusionment that comes with having to make such unplanned, uncertain transitions can fill you with fear and feelings of betrayal from your previous place.

Other times, when you are not leaving, you are being forced out without a good cause. This often leaves you discouraged and paralyzed by the shame and confusion of having to suffer for something you not only didn't plan but can barely even understand.

The result of turbulent transitions always leave you surprised. The array of emotions that characterize these transitions make it more difficult to handle, for how do you get yourself to believe that God is in control of something that almost wrecked you?

The complications of turbulent transitions tend to leave people broken, filled with pain, and heartless, so much so that they resort to becoming sources of pain to others.

The overwhelming nature of such transitions is fuelled by the numerous unanswered questions that plague the hearts of those who go through it. During these seasons, you would require more intentional levels of patience and humility, enough to understand that, despite the invitation to oneness with God, He still holds the rights of sovereignty.

Although, sometimes, He doesn't give you an explanation for your experiences, He expects you to walk in wisdom, knowing that, in all, He is working out His purpose in you.

In addition to humility and patience, you need a level of responsibility to accept that your transition is also causing a transition in others. Your need to leave your previous season causes a void that would cause them to deploy strategies to manage the transition they have come into, as a result of your transition.

In an act of service, you need to understand how your transition affects the people and systems of your previous season and let that guide how you steward it. It takes your ability to appreciate the value and impact of your previous season to hold yourself accountable and regard them honorably, although being true to the need to transition.

The dynamics of transition are such that you might have to go through smaller transitions while working toward the whole process transition.

> *"You might have to go through smaller transitions while working towards the whole transition"*

In God's attempt to bring you into the new season, He might move to teach you about your finances, show you how to manage people, help you understand the fullness of what He is calling you to do and other things, and what you need to succeed is humility.

The humility to accept that you are walking through an unfamiliar path, in need of God and guidance, which would require you to keep your eyes and ears open and your mouth shut to glean the wisdom and voice of God without interference.

Since you need to make transitions, you must test every spirit to be certain that you are not listening to your fears and the projections of other people appearing as God, because of how they resonate with your emotions. Transitions are not fruits of misgivings or a mere response to your biases, lest they lead you astray, no matter how convinced you may be.

You must be careful to not 'put words in God's mouth' out of your experience with your current season. God only backs His Word, and where you are not walking in line with the Word, you can as well retrace your steps in repentance, which in itself starts a new transition in righteousness.

In transitions, you are more likely to be led by your emotions rather than submit to God's perspective, which leaves you in pursuit of convenience over the will of God.

> *“God backs only His Word”*

All things might work together for good, in the end, but there is more to God than His good will. There is also the perfect will of God, which usually requires more pruning, and subjects you to a process where you yield your will to Him, seeing how incompetent you are in the face of the challenge.

**TRANSITION RATIONALIZATION**

Transition rationalization is the practice of strategically identifying systems or patterns in your life, to determine which of them should be kept, replaced, retired, or consolidated. This process can help you to achieve improvement in your overall function and to make better use of your time and resources.

By engaging in transition rationalization, you can identify areas of your life that are not serving you well, and make changes that will help you to thrive.

For example, you might identify patterns of behavior or thinking that are holding you back or systems that are inefficient or ineffective. By replacing or retiring these patterns or systems, you can create space for advancement. Here are three ways that transition Rationalization can improve your overall function:

- By engaging in transition rationalization, you can identify patterns or systems in your life that are not serving you well, and make changes to eliminate or replace them. This can include patterns of behavior or thinking that are holding you back, as well as inefficient or ineffective systems.

> *"Identify areas of your life that are not serving you well, and make changes that will help you to thrive"*

- By eliminating these patterns or systems, you can free up time, energy, and resources, and can focus on the things that are most important to you.
- Transition rationalization can help you to optimize your use of resources, including your time, energy, and money. By evaluating the systems and patterns in your life, you can identify areas where you are wasting resources and can make changes to be more efficient and effective.

For example, you might identify patterns of behavior or thinking that are causing you to waste time or energy, or you might identify systems that are inefficient or costly to maintain.

- By optimizing your use of resources, you can achieve

more with less, and can better align your lives with your goals and values.

However, there are seven (7) risks associated with not engaging in accurate transition rationalization, including:

**-HOLDING ON TO LOW-VALUE PROPOSITIONS**

By clinging to systems or patterns that no longer serve you well, you may be holding on to low-value propositions that are not worth your time or energy. This can be especially costly if you are wasting time trying to defend a wrong decision that you have made.

> *"Create space for growth and improvement in your life"*

**-BEING UNABLE TO PLAN, OPTIMIZE, AND GROW DIFFERENT ASPECTS OF YOUR LIFE**

If you are unable to engage in transition rationalization, you may struggle to plan, optimize, and grow in different aspects of your life. You may find yourself stuck in patterns or systems that are no longer serving you well, and may be unable to adapt to new situations or challenges. This can prevent you from achieving your full potential and from reaching your goals.

**-AN INCREASED COST OF FULFILLING PURPOSE**

Any existing aspect of your life that reduces the lubrication of grace in your life becomes a liability to the manifestation of your purpose. This can be incredibly challenging if you are trying to fulfil your calling or intent, as it may require you to give up things that you value or things that have constituted your identity.

The increased cost of fulfilling your purpose implies the need to exercise both vigilance and caution in your transition rationalization to avoid incurring additional costs in your efforts to achieve your goals and fulfil your purpose. This can occur if you are unable to react promptly to changing conditions.

For example, if you are latched on to a belief or approach that is no longer helpful or relevant, you may find that it hinders your progress and prevents you from moving forward effectively.

Imagine you're a person who has always believed that asking for help is a sign of weakness. You have internalized the idea that you should be self-sufficient and handle your problems independently. This belief has been ingrained in you from a young age, perhaps due to cultural or personal experiences.

As you navigate through life, you encounter various challenges and hardships. Instead of reaching out for support, you internalize your struggles and attempt to bear the burden alone. You put on a brave face and hide your vulnerability, believing that asking for help would make you appear inadequate or dependent.

> *"Every time there is an aspect of your life that reduces the lubrication of grace in your life, it is a cost to your purpose"*

Over time, this belief starts taking a toll on your emotional well-being. You feel overwhelmed, isolated, and emotionally drained. The weight of your problems becomes too heavy to bear on your own, but you continue to resist seeking assistance out of fear or pride.

As a result, you find yourself trapped in a cycle of emotional distress. Your mental health suffers, and you struggle to maintain healthy relationships. Your progress in personal and professional areas of life becomes hindered, as you lack the support and guidance that could help you overcome obstacles and grow.

Imagine the drain this can have on your resources. The divine energy and grace allotted per time and season for launching ahead is instead expended playing catch up or attempting to recover from missed opportunities. It then becomes a weary and cumbersome process trying to attain the goals of the new day or season.

> *"Our loyalty to men is based on our loyalty to God"*

## AFRAID OF WHAT YOU MIGHT FIND

There are several reasons why you might be afraid of what you will chance upon when it comes to asking difficult questions about your transitions. Four (4) possible reasons include:

1. **Fear of Change:** Most people generally have an unwillingness to adapt to altered circumstances. Change appears intimidating and can be scary, and many people are afraid of what the future may hold. Asking difficult questions about your transition may generate some insecurity and anxiety which can be uncomfortable.

2. **Fear of Failure:** You may be afraid of the realization of having made mistakes. or that your best-laid plans are not unfolding in the way you envisioned them. This fear of failure can be a barrier to initiating brutally honest conversations, asking tough questions, and seeking critical assistance and guidance

that may be needed to ensure that you are on the right path.

3. **Fear of Confrontation:** Asking difficult questions may involve confronting yourself, or others or going against the grain of societal culture which can be daunting. You may be apprehensive about the reaction of others and the consequences of their actions.

4. **Fear of Vulnerability:** Asking tough questions often necessitates a substantial degree of vulnerability which often leaves the unnerving sentiment of feeling exposed.

   It is very probable that you are afraid of being judged or rejected if you reveal your doubts or weaknesses.

## YOU ARE GIVING AWAY MORE THAN YOU ARE RECEIVING.

> *"If you feel that you are always being misunderstood, as it may mean that you are with people who won't understand your journey or your goals"*

Relationships are generally meant to function in a symbiotic way, however, if not engaged with discernment and caution, you may find yourself giving away more than you are receiving in your relationship and interactions. You may wind up leaking grace, strength, and opportunities, and may be leaving yourself vulnerable to being taken advantage of or used.

It is crucial to address the fear of realizing that you are giving away more than you are receiving because it can have a significant impact on your overall well-being and happiness. When you feel like you are not getting enough in return for your efforts, it can be emotionally and physically draining and may lead to resentment and conflict. This can take a toll on your mental and physical health and may make it harder to achieve your goals and live a fulfilling life.

By addressing this fear, you can establish healthy boundaries and create more balance in your relationships and situations.

Here are two (2) benefits of addressing the fear of giving away more than you are receiving:

1. **Stronger relationships:** When you establish healthy boundaries and create more balance in your relationships, you can build stronger and more positive connections with others. This can improve your overall satisfaction and happiness.
2. **Greater fulfilment:** By focusing on what is most important to you and ensuring that you are getting enough in return for your efforts, you can achieve greater fulfilment and satisfaction in your life.

## YOU RISK MISSING YOUR DESTINY ALTOGETHER

Finally, the most dangerous risk associated with not engaging in transition rationalization is the very likely possibility of having a repackaged destiny altogether. If you are unable to discern the next move of God or align with it, you will lose out on the opportunities and blessings that were intended for you.

There are three (3) ways in which people can risk missing out on their destinies by failing to carefully rationalize their seasons of transition:

1. **By not paying attention to God's guidance:** During a season of transition, it is important to listen carefully to God's guidance and to be open to His leading. If you are not careful

in your transition rationalization, you may miss out on opportunities or make decisions that are not in alignment with God's plan for your life.

The tendency to freestyle difficult seasons of your life out of the fear of being vulnerable will only cost you more. It could even be the purpose of subjecting you to such seasons, to help you discover God's guidance in intimacy and learning from others. If you fail to yield to this, you are likely to lead yourself away from God's plan for your life.

2. **By not adapting to changing circumstances:** As the changes happen, gradually or suddenly, if you are unable to react promptly to changing circumstances, you may miss out on opportunities or find yourself in difficult situations.

3. **By not letting go of the past:** One truth that will guide you to the next phase of your life is acknowledging that there were limitations in your past or current level that cannot birth the fullness of God's will for you. Regardless of how you might have handled the past seasons of your life, by the privilege of grace, you must accept every opportunity to let go of the past and embrace the present. If you are holding onto past mistakes or regrets, it can be difficult to move forward and realize your destiny.

## REDEFINING RELATIONSHIPS AND LOYALTY

As you go through transitions, you may find that your relationships and loyalties are tested and redefined. It is important to remember that our loyalty to men is based on our loyalty to God and that we may need to adjust our relationships and loyalties as we move through different seasons of our lives.

For example, you may find that you are no longer able to rely on certain relationships or connections that you have had in the past and that you need to build new relationships or connections to support your current goals and needs.

This can be a challenging process, as it may require you to let go of old patterns or habits and forge new relationships and connections that are more in line with your current vision and purpose.

You may also find out that you are misunderstood or misjudged by those around you, as you go through transitions. This can be especially frustrating if you feel that you are always being misunderstood, as it may mean that you are with people who won't understand your journey or your goals. In these situations, while we may have many relationships and loyalties that are important to us, ultimately, our loyalty to God should be the foundation upon which all of our other relationships and loyalties are built.

Following a successful transition rationalization, here are five (5) steps you can take to block leakages that could be jeopardizing your transition:

1. Identify The Leakages: Take some time to assess your current situation and identify any areas where you may be leaking grace, strength, or opportunities. This may involve looking at your habits, relationships, finances, or other areas of your life.
2. Set Specific Goals: Determine what changes you would like to make to block the leakages and set specific, achievable goals for yourself. For example, you might set a goal to improve your financial management or to develop healthier

relationships.

3. Seek Support: It can be helpful to seek support from others, such as friends, family, or a therapist, as you work to block the leakages. They can provide encouragement and accountability as you work toward your goals.

4. Make A Plan: Develop a plan for how you will implement the changes you need to make. This may involve setting aside specific times to work on your goals or finding ways to make positive choices more convenient.

5. Be Patient and Persistent: Changing habits and patterns can be difficult, and it is important to be patient with yourself. If you encounter setbacks, don't be discouraged –just keep working toward your goals and be persistent.

However, it is important to recognize that transition rationalization is not a one-time process, but rather a continuous cycle of evaluation and adjustment.

## *Chapter 3*

# THE BIG PICTURE

*You have to understand that who you are is usually a product of the people you've been with, the places you've been, and the situations you've faced over the years.*

*Chapter 3*

# THE BIG PICTURE

Our life journey is like a plane that eventually taxies to a point of great reckoning where it becomes glaringly obvious that whatever we are currently experiencing is a result of a combination of factors that we experienced or encountered in the past.

There are several ways in which life is unravelled and how we deal with those previous scenes and episodes of life largely determines who we become in the current season of life.

> *"Everyone, including you, has a story that defines their existence."*

Everyone, including you has a story that defines their existence. That story will do one of two things; it is either fortifying you so you face life with power or destroying you by making you avoid challenges. You have to understand that who you are is a product of the people you've been with, the places you've been, and the situations you've faced over the years.

To understand what you are experiencing, you must understand how you got to where you are now. These three factors got you this far, and they will determine how much you can achieve this season.

## PEOPLE IN YOUR LIFE

Don't be ignorant of how much influence the people in your life have on you. To put it mildly, everything you know and do today is something you learned from someone else. You also need to understand that these people are moulding you into the value of the lessons they add to your life, whether negative or positive.

Growing up in Nigeria, we were used to parents with big, lofty dreams for us to fulfil, parents who wanted us to become doctors, lawyers, or engineers. This left me wondering why they wanted these things for us so much.

> *"Everything you know and do today is something you learned from someone else"*

It was rather unusual to have parents who deviated from this school of thought. I dare say this thinking that "successful" children had to attain this set of "respectable careers" did most of us more harm than good. Several seeds of unique creative expressions were buried before they ever had a chance to sprout as we all dutifully towed this cookie cutter pattern laid out for us. In my own case, I was unable to fully explore and unleash the depths of my curiosity and creativity as a child. I remember when my eldest son, Nathan, got creatively busy enough to write a book. I am not sure what exactly inspired him to write a book when he was seven years old, but it was certainly a piece that expressed the beauty and wisdom of a seven-year- old.

After the elation that came with it, he handed over the book to me. I was proud of his accomplishments but regrettably, I kept the book in the archives. It took a while for God to make me understand what my actions could potentially translate into; One day, the Holy Spirit reminded me of this. If I bought into my son's vision to promote his book and support him in that regard, he would have written more books or pursued his other passions. That was when it dawned on me that it matters who oversees your creativity.

You could either be discouraged from growing in your areas of strength and influence by people who cannot understand where God is leading you or you may meet people who are doing their best to support and enhance your growth.

*Mark 6:7 (NIV):*

*"Calling the Twelve to him, he began to send them out two by two and gave them authority over impure spirits."*

When Jesus met fishermen and tax collectors, He saw more than what they were doing. He did not only see what they would become, but He also freed them from their condition, held their hands, taught and empowered them to fulfill their destinies.

After Jesus taught His disciples orally and by being an example of what he wanted to achieve through them, He realized that this would not be enough. It wasn't enough for Him to give them power or the Holy Spirit. He took it upon himself to strategically put them on the field, giving them experiential knowledge to reach and grow in their potential. The results of His actions not only affected the disciples who were liberated and healed but also increased their confidence in themselves and in what they had received.

*Mark 6:13 (NIV):*

*"They drove out many demons and anointed many sick people with oil and healed them."*

Why do you think Peter and John were able to help the man at the beautiful gate?

*Acts 3:1-7 (NIV):*

*"One day Peter and John were going up to the temple at the time of prayer—at three in the afternoon. Now a man who was lame from birth was being carried to the temple gate called Beautiful, where he was put every day to beg from those going into the temple courts. When he saw Peter and John about to enter, he asked them for money. Peter looked straight at him, as did John. Then Peter said, "Look at us!" So the man gave them his attention, expecting to get something from them. Then Peter said, "Silver*

*or gold I do not have, but what I do have I give you. In the name of Jesus Christ of Nazareth, walk." Taking him by the right hand, he helped him up, and instantly the man's feet and ankles became strong."*

> *"Never become familiar with those who God has positioned to take you through this season"*

This wasn't a mere display of the fruit of power but a product of confidence built through experience. It wasn't the first time they would use the name of Jesus to bring help to people in need. Jesus had them test the power long enough to prove its efficacy and rid their hearts of every doubt, so much so that when the time came to stand up to responsibility, they responded from a place of confidence. The secret isn't in the power they possessed but it is in the training Jesus subjected them to. How you respond to what is happening will be determined by how you have been taught to respond.

If I don't actively renew my support for my son's creativity, that part of him may become dormant until God stirs him up later in life. He will go about knowing he has all it takes to excel in that area, but wouldn't know why he's unable to explore his gift.

> *"The limitations of your environment become the scope of your possibilities"*

The people around you give you the opportunities, energy, and time to identify and shape your purpose, and you must learn how to leverage them as your greatest asset and vehicle for transition.

People can facilitate the success of your transition, the reality is that people carry seasons, and what influence they bring is determined by the season they represent. As they come into your life, they bring a new season and certain conditions that can catalyze or inhibit your transition process.

In order not to jeopardize the integrity of your transition by associating with those who are likely to inhibit or corrupt your process, you must sustain the relevant discernment to understand the season's people carry and to perceive them beyond their appearance.

When you identify those whose presence tend to catalyze your transition, you must understand that they are also in a transition.

There is no real assurance that they will stay beyond the present, but to gain their prolonged commitment to you and your journey, you must equally find ways and opportunities to contribute to their process. Don't be the one who is always in need of help, instead remain ever ready to extend support to others when it is in your power to do so.

> *"There's only so much you can do trying to build on a weak foundation"*

While people around you can connect you to the knowledge, skills, strategies and people you need to go through this season successfully, you must nevertheless resist with all your might the natural tendency to descend into familiarity with those who God has positioned to take you through this season. Familiarity, both in terms of having contempt for the blessings God brings to you and building your transition around such people.

Your relationship with them should help you develop new skills, exposure, experience and empower you with the resources to refine your direction and boost your journey. The relationship should reshape your goals for the transition, based on the new level of exposure that you have, rather than abandon your transition to settle for what the relationship offers.

As you relate with people during this season of transition, be circumspect so that you don't choose your company based on what you feel they have to offer, instead your choice should be hinged to the unity of purpose, integrity and trust.

You will meet people who might not seem helpful today, but could become your Saviour tomorrow, and what matters is your ability to create a lasting relationship with people as they come. Find ways to enrich the relationship by making relevant contributions to their journey, to create the opportunity for the flow of value from them.

**THE PLACES YOU HAVE BEEN**

Our physical environment has the power to define our potential. Even Jesus was prone to being labelled by the limitations of his environment.

*John 1:45-46 (NIV):*

*"Philip found Nathaniel and told him, 'We have found the one Moses wrote about in the Law, and about whom the prophets also wrote—Jesus of Nazareth, the son of Joseph. Nazareth! Can anything good come from there?' Nathaniel asked. 'Come and see,' said Philip."*

There was nothing sentimental about Nathaniel's statement. He was just stating the obvious, and not even Philip disputed it. All Philip could say was that he was so astonished by the reality of the blessing from Nazareth that he decided to show it to him.

Far from what you might have imagined, Jesus wasn't defensive about it. He knew that Nathaniel was being true to history, as a devout Israelite, from His statement in John 1:47 *"When Jesus saw Nathaniel approaching, He said of him, 'Here truly is an Israelite in whom there is no deceit.'"*

The places you have been to inform your perspective about what is possible within a certain sphere of operation as well as what is not. The consequential perspective you then hold has the power to make or break you in matters pertaining to destiny.

Have you tried to imagine why God insisted on raising Moses as one who would deliver Israel from the oppression in Egypt?

*Exodus 3:10 (NIV):*

*"So now, go. I am sending you to Pharaoh to bring my people the Israelites out of Egypt."*

When Moses declined and suggested that God should use someone else for obvious reasons, why didn't God do away with him?

> *"Your transition is either nourished or frustrated by the places you find yourself"*

*Exodus 4:13*

*"But Moses said, 'Pardon your servant, Lord. Please send someone else.'"*

Why did God engage Moses in a debate to make him understand the purpose and power of the task and why Moses had to go? To confront the Pharaoh-the symbol of your oppression, requires more than just having a great calling.

The answer is simple. Moses grew up in the palace. He was used to Egyptian wisdom and surely didn't consider Pharaoh as his oppressor.

Surely, it would have taken longer than the 40 years Moses spent in the wilderness to train slaves (the Israelites in Egypt) to have the confidence to tell the truth to power. The conditioning a slave would have undergone during a difficult oppressive process would have influenced his manner of approaching Pharaoh and his response to the pushbacks in the face of pressure.

> "*To see life from a perspective that transcends your present state, you must fight for spiritual supremacy*"

Moses stood up to Pharaoh with the support of Jehovah coupled with his advantageous experience of palace culture. If he had been inspired by a noble desire to be a freedom fighter, motivated by the sheer support of the people, he would have been frustrated, because they were discouraged by the idea.

-Exodus6:9

*"Moses reported this to the Israelites, but they did not listen to him because of their discouragement and harsh labor."*

Ever wondered why Moses was unaffected even when Pharaoh ordered the Israelites to work under worse conditions? Even when Pharaoh's men also turned their wands into snakes, it took the experience to keep Moses from running away.

Being in Egypt empowered him to confront what was before him with courage, even though courage meant going back to God for strength and direction. Likewise, the places you have been to and been bred in are usually the places and conditions that can build or break your destiny.

Within the places you have been are usually the people and conditions that greatly influenced your destiny to the point where your definitions of good and bad, possibility and impossibility are affected. These places create a mental picture and become the canvas upon which you paint your future. Truth be told, no matter how well intentioned your motives, or how noble your plans may be, there's really very little progress made attempting to build on a weak foundation.

Your transition is either nourished or frustrated by the places you find yourself, because they determine who you meet and the resultant experiences. By virtue of being in a place, you become influenced by its culture, and the scope of your vision isn't left out, because the limitations of your environment become your comfort zone.

Beyond the conventional obvious spiritual attacks, the forces that control territories put systems and structures in place to govern the mindset and culture of those within, to the extent that your perspective on life is defined by the forces that influence the environment you are in.

These forces put pressure on what you know and your quest for solution, thereby threatening the success of your transition.

Despite the existence of these forces, the good news is that we are designed and positioned in Christ to take advantage of our environment. We have been called to dominate, and to live above the culture of the places we have been.

## THE CONDITIONS YOU HAVE EXPERIENCED

The places you have been and the people you have been with create the situations and events that drive you to act the way you do. Whether it is Jesus and His disciples, my son and I, Moses and Egypt, they all help to lead you to the fulfilment of your destiny or keep you away from it.

These conditions may be created by others, like the case of my son, it may be orchestrated by God, as in Moses, or intentionally, as in the case of Jesus and his disciples.

Being with people or places that subject you to abuse or other forms of mistreatment may be due to an obsession with your desires. Like the children of Israel in slavery, their condition left them far removed from God's promises. You have to accept that locked into the conditions you have been through are seasons, resources, and 'beasts' you'll have to contend with.

Each condition is an opportunity to grow into the person God created you to be, or to step away from the path of destiny. To see life from a perspective that transcends your present state, you must fight for spiritual supremacy. To effectively navigate what you are going through, you must find God's perspective that contradicts your negative experience, and you have to accept it as God's plan for your life.

Here are seven ways to channel the experiences you have gained from people, places, and conditions to make successful transitions:

1. **Reflect on your experiences:** Take some time to reflect on the experiences you have had and consider what you have learned from them. What lessons can you draw from your interactions with people, your experiences in different places, and the conditions you have encountered?

2. **Identify your strengths and areas for growth:** Consider your strengths and areas for growth in light of your experiences. What skills or qualities have you developed that can help you navigate your transition successfully? What areas might you need to work on in order to achieve your goals?

3. **Set specific goals:** Determine what you want to achieve in your transition and set specific, achievable goals for yourself. This can help you to focus your efforts and stay motivated as you work toward your desired outcomes.

4. **Seek support:** Consider seeking support from others, such as friends, family, or a therapist, as you work to make your transition a success. They can provide encouragement, guidance, and accountability as you work toward your goals.

5. **Be open to learning:** Be open to learning from your experiences and from others as you navigate your transition. This may involve seeking out new opportunities for learning or feedback from others to help you improve and grow.

6. **Reflect on your ancestry:** Take some time to reflect on your ancestry and consider the ways in which it has shaped your beliefs, values, and behaviors. What are the

strengths and limitations of your ancestry, and how might they be impacting your current situation?

7. **Identify limiting beliefs:** Consider whether you have any limiting beliefs or patterns of thought that are rooted in your ancestry that may be holding you back. These may include negative self-perceptions, fears, or limiting assumptions about what is possible for you.

*Chapter 4*

# THE STRATEGY OF HELL

*The reality is not about what you want, but what you have become as a result of your experiences.*

# Chapter 4

# THE STRATEGY OF HELL

There is a location in the realm of the spirit that is like a memory bank of experiences. You can decide the state of that memory bank by the way you handle a matter spiritually, knowing that the same God that can cause light to come out of darkness can also cause good to come out of any and every situation in our lives and memories.

God can and will strengthen us, but we need to take a position concerning the various matters that we are faced with. The taking of a position in the spirit doesn't happen all at once, it will always take time. The key to living that way is to continually surrender the good, the bad, and the ugly to God. As long as you do this, Satan cannot use your experiences as weapons or ammunition against you in the future.

*"You need to be willing to look at your family history and the patterns you have inherited, and be willing to make changes"*

Part of the things that Satan does is to remind you of your past failures when you have arrived at a boundary of transition where God is about to bring you into promotion, increase, and a new realm of engagement. When you have arrived at a boundary of transition where God is about to bring you into promotion, increase, and a new realm of engagement —he will start reminding you of your past failures.

Satan reminds you of your shortcomings to weaken your conviction and ability to seize and live in a "New day."". It is a systemic programming of hell so that even if you are never attacked by the devil in the next 15 years, he can bank on the programming to bring you down. He will ensure that you keep self-sabotaging.

> *"Do not be satisfied with the crumbs that make your situation seem a bit good"*

Another way that Satan propagates this programming is to engage and lock multiple generations into a carousel of curses. Round and round, the family goes from cycle to cycle and pattern to pattern of recurring issues with each generation becoming the strength of the chain that binds the next generation stronger to the curse. Another definition of a *'curse'* is to be *'lightweight'*. When we talk about a *"curse"* being *"lightweight,"* we mean that it is something that doesn't feel like a big deal or something that we can easily ignore. This could refer to a range of issues that can be passed down through generations, such as patterns of behavior, beliefs, or values.

The problem is that when these "lightweight" issues are passed down from generation to generation, they can become stronger and more deeply ingrained in each new generation. For example, if a family has a history of unhealthy coping mechanisms like avoidance or denial, this could become a pattern that is passed down from parents to children, with each new generation picking up the habit and making it more difficult to break.

Over time, as these patterns become more deeply ingrained, they start to feel like the norm. If you grew up in an environment where certain behaviors or attitudes are accepted or even encouraged, you may not realize that there are other ways of being or thinking.

This is why the fourth generation of the family may not even know what they're *"warring against."* They don't recognize that there's a problem because it is has become so normalized.

Breaking this cycle of *"lightweight"* curses requires awareness and intentionality. You need to be willing to look at your family history and the patterns you have inherited, and be willing to make changes.

This might involve seeking out therapy or counselling, learning new coping strategies, or challenging our own beliefs and assumptions. It can be a difficult and uncomfortable process, but it is important to go through the process in order to prevent these *"lightweight"* curses from becoming even more deeply ingrained in future generations.

> *"The things you are stimulated by will become the things that define your path"*

Hell strengthens the lightness in one generation, thereby making another generation even lighter, till the fourth generation arrives at the point where they do not know the things to war against and they think it is normal. The reason why Satan implements this programming is so that in the day you are called to a place of influence and authority, your mind starts to question whether it can carry that kind of path that God has set for you, you are unable to walk in them because Satan would have locked your mind into a mentality of smallness and incapacity. Satan He creates boundaries around how much you can do per time. This is how he programs people and does it through generations. The process is usually facilitated by satanic structures around regions, systems, and even sometimes, families.

> *"Prayer is the tool that massages the truth into the soul"*

Those who are locked within this lobe become satisfied with whatever they are given and count the slightest crumbs thrown their way as a blessing.

Is there more? Then, cry out for more.

Is it possible to contend for the greater things? Then cry out for the greater things. Do not be satisfied with the crumbs that make your situation seem a bit good -that is a programming hell. Darkness usually strengthens this experience by ensuring that there is a thorn in your flesh that serves as a constant reminder of your captivity.

Hell uses this campaign strategy to remove from the mind of its victim, the thought and possibility of escape - what such a person begins to do is plan their life around that captivity. They make and take pivotal decisions such as who to marry, and the number of children to have, to accommodate that captivity, so that you are safe within the confines of oppression. What a travesty for those who have been made co-heirs of Christ! This is how hell works. The reason for this is so that you are never able to make the necessary leaps that God has got in store for you. When you get born again, your spirit is saved, and your soul is also saved but because the soul is the seat of our emotions and passions, many things need to be refined by God.

Your spirit merely goes on a journey of getting to know and grow in the Lord, but your soul is the one that has actively engaged in this world so your soul needs to be reborn and re-taught how to desire the way God desires, how to interpret the way God interprets and how to feel the way God feels.

There is a new teaching that goes on with your soul, and the soul is what sits between the spirit and the body. Many times, it feels like there is a constant contention between the body and the spirit for the soul. The body is constantly in a place where it tries to get the soul to desire what it desires- to feel good, drink, eat late at night, etc., and it wants the soul to be set in what it wants, but the spirit is in disagreement with the body and dictates what the soul should desire.

> *"There is a level of strength and audacity that you need to embrace the opportunities of God"*

You will always move in the direction of your passion, and this is why you must steward your soul very carefully with the things you will allow to stimulate you. The things you are stimulated by become the things that you are passionate about.The cure for the struggles in the soul is the truth of the spirit, and prayer is the way to move transport the truth from the spirit to the soul. Use prayer to massage the truth into the soul.

Sometimes, the soul is like a rebel that wants to go wherever it is pulled but you need to have the spirit remind it that it belongs to a family that is subject to Christ, and it is in the place of prayer that you take these matters to the Lord.

Take the word you hear and speak it over your soul, commanding your spirit, soul and body to march forward and arrive at the throne of God. When all three of them are at the throne, begin to declare so that there is no part of you that doesn't reflect the will, power and glory of God. The realities that your spirit comes into, your soul comes into the same.

> *“We have trained ourselves so much to hear only the rebukes of God and not the praises of God”*

You must develop and maintain consistency in prayer. So many people pray spiritual prayers but they do not allow these spiritual prayers to break down the concepts within the realms of their souls. When something is highlighted to you by God to deal with, bring it before Him consistently in prayer and over time you will realize that the struggles will be broken. As a result of constant prayer and deliberately starving the soul of worldly emotions, the soul becomes trained to desire the things of Christ.

Even the body has an inheritance in heaven, therefore every part of your needs to recognize the voice of God but it is you that must take them and subject them to the voice of the Lord.

Unfortunately, Satan has propagated the false gospel of false humility throughout the church so you find that many Christians who were bold and audacious when they were in the world become timid when they receive Christ. Have now become timid. They lose lost their courage and audacity the moment they become became believers and that is not God's way of operation.

Look at the people God used to spread the Gospel of Christ, even when He converted their spirit. Paul was still a man of audacity, going from city to city, standing in front of Pilate, still having the same zeal to do the things which he did when he was in the world but now for Christ.Also, in the same vein, Rahab, in spite of her status as a prostitute was used by God to birth a powerful deliverance. We also note with admiration how adeptly she negotiated for the salvation of her lineage, and remarkably, God never questioned her audacity but instead met her requests. There is a level of strength and audacity that you need to be able to embrace the opportunities of God, but what stops you from doing that is the little seeds of doubt and low self-esteem that the enemy has sown into our minds. Imagine if Rahab allowed people's opinions to get to her, she never wouldn't have asked and then she never would have received and changed the destiny of her entire lineage. Same with David when he slew Goliath, he first negotiated before he slew the giant.

> *"The Lord doesn't need you to be safe, the Lord needs you to trust Him"*

The boldness and audacity of God's spirit can be present in you so that when you come into a season of crossing, you can, like

Elisha, you can take Elijah's mantle and strike the Jordan. Who told Elisha that the river Jordan would part for him? Elisha must have thought to himself that for the mantle to fall where he was and for the Lord to permit him to carry it, then he could can handle it.

> *"Many people have lost opportunities because they kept highlighting the things they were not as opposed to the things that they are"*

We need to confront the things that need to be confronted and come into the place where we are saturated by the presence of God in every realm of our existence. Only then can we truly make the necessary transitions.

What's the difference between true audacity and over- inflated importance? The Holy Ghost and Truth. The Holy Spirit is the Spirit of Truth, so He brings you into all truth, however, some people have the Holy Spirit but do not allow the Holy Ghost to speak His truth, especially if the truth is confronting or going against everything you have ever known in the world and in the faith.

The Holy Spirit will always tell you if it isn't God, but He the Holy Spirit will sometimes challenge the things that you have defined as humility. We have trained ourselves so much to hear only the rebukes of God and not His the praises of God, so when God praises us, it is uncomfortable because we always expect him to rebuke us.

In our strong humanity, we fail to allow ourselves to trust God. It is impossible to make the necessary transitions in life if you do not trust the Father, but to trust the Father, you need to know the Father. You need to know that He is faithful and can be trusted.

Some of us have father trauma from our earthly fathers. The problem is that we try to mirror our relationship with the Heavenly Father through the experience of our relationships with our earthly fathers but how can you qualify the whole from the broken? But instead, you should qualify the broken using the whole as the standard.

You cannot know God as a father through the lenses of the physical fathers —you must first know God as the father and standard of fatherhood. Then we can evaluate the other fathers in our lives. It doesn't matter if you never had it; allow God to be the father to you.

Do not be afraid to fail because the fact that you are failing is evidence that you are still making moves, trying, pushing the boundaries, and growing in the process. The Lord doesn't need you to be safe, the Lord needs you to trust Him, and neither does He need you to get it excellently but to move when He says move. In the midst of transitions, just keep your eye on the Father —that's how you make successful transitions.

**THE MEPHIBOSHETH SYNDROME**

*2 Samuel 4:4,*

*"Jonathan, son of Saul, had a son who was lame in both feet. He was five years old when the news about Saul and Jonathan came from Jezreel. His nurse picked him up and fled, but as she hurried to leave, he fell and became disabled. His name was Mephibosheth."*

*2 Samuel 9:1-12;*

*"David asked, "Is there anyone still left of the house of Saul to whom I can show kindness for Jonathan's sake?" Now there was a servant of Saul's household named Ziba. They summoned him to appear before David, and the king said to him, "Are you Ziba?" "At your service," he replied. The king asked, "Is there no one still alive from the house of Saul to whom I can show God's kindness?" Ziba answered the king, "There is still a son of Jonathan; he is lame in both feet." "Where is he?" the king asked.*

*Ziba answered, "He is at the house of Makir son of Ammiel in Lo Debar." So King David had him brought from Lo Debar, from the house of Makir son of Ammiel. When Mephibosheth son of Jonathan, the son of Saul, came to David, he bowed down to pay him honor. David said, "Mephibosheth!" "At your service," he replied. "Don't be afraid," David said to him, "for I will surely show you kindness for the sake of your father Jonathan. I will restore to you all the land that belonged to your grandfather Saul, and you will always eat at my table." Mephibosheth bowed down and said, "What is your servant, that you should notice a dead dog like me?" Then the king summoned Ziba, Saul's steward, and said to him, "I have given your master's grandson everything that belonged to Saul and his family. You and your sons and your servants are to farm the land for him and bring in the crops, so that your master's grandson may be provided for. And Mephibosheth, grandson of your master, will always eat at my table." (Now Ziba had fifteen sons and twenty servants.) Then Ziba said to the king, "Your servant will do whatever my lord the king commands his servant to do." So Mephibosheth ate at David's table like one of the king's sons. Mephibosheth had a young son named Mika, and all the members of Ziba's household were servants of Mephibosheth. And Mephibosheth lived in Jerusalem, because he always ate at the king's table; he was lame in both feet."*

This is the story of a man who was meant to be a prince but he thought of himself as a dead dog.

Mephibosheth means exterminating the idols; he was destined to be the one used by God to take down the idols in his lineage/ generation. But tragedy hit his father and brother, and while he was being taken away by his nurse, he fell from her hands, broke his legs, and became lame.

From being the grandson of Saul and the son of Jonathan, he went into a place called Lodebar which means *'not a pasture'*.' He went from living in a palace to living in a dry land, a dead place. Mephibosheth made a transition that was not of God.

It was set up by hell and darkness, and one of the first things that the enemy did was to cripple his legs so that he could not move or escape Lodebar. This way he had to constantly depend on people for help to be taken around. He went from being a prince who had the liberty of running around the palace and exploring all that the king has got for him, to being a person who was born to take down the idols, he became subject to a dry land to the extent that he lost his identity.

> *". If you are deserving to sit at God's table, then why aren't you deserving to sit at the table of the kings of this earth?"*

When the king shows up to bless him, he wonders what the king wants from him because he believes himself to be a dead dog—undeserving of the king's attention and blessing. If David did not force the movement and transition on him, Mephibosheth would have lived and died in Lodebar.

Many people have Mephibosheth Syndrome; the day that the king sends for them, they are quick to remind the king of their inadequacies —both the spiritual King of all creations and the kings of this world. Many people have lost opportunities because they kept highlighting the things they were not, as opposed to the things that they are. The Mephibosheth Syndrome makes it hard for people to transition into the things that the Lord has got for them and allocated for them.

The thing about your transition is that the Lord will inspire the people He has sent to you for that reason, but you have to obey and go with the flow. The moment God put David in that situation, it was now in Mephibosheth's hand. What will you do with that situation, Mephibosheth? We understand the weaknesses; broken legs and being lame, but the Lord is saying it is time to shift, and enter into the new life. What will your response be? The other people David favored were given places and areas to work in, but Mephibosheth's was to sit at the king's table, just sit.

> *"You do not need to tell them what they do not need to hear"*

Imagine how rich the king's table is, with royals and nobles who must have wondered who Mephibosheth was and how he gained a seat at the table, but the king doesn't care about that because when he looks at Mephibosheth, he doesn't see lameness and broken legs, or the failed attempts at walking but what the king sees is who Mephibosheth is on the inside, the son of Jonathan. David loved Mephibosheth through the love he had for Jonathan. In the same way, God loves us through the love that He has for Jesus. The promises of God to you aren't because of who you are; there's nothing you can do to win it, but because of who Christ is, and as a son of Jesus, you deserve to sit at God's table.

If you are deserving to sit at God's table, then why aren't you deserving to sit at the table of the kings of this earth? If the God of the whole earth can call you up despite your lame legs, why would you think that any king of this world has the right to disqualify you because of that very same lameness?

Some people have not transitioned in the way that they should because they are constantly reminded of the things they are not. Sometimes even those who should care for us (our nurses) will wound us unintentionally, sometimes they will break us—nurses of mentors, rulers, gatekeepers over our lives, and in trying to save us and do the best for us through their weaknesses, they may break us. However, Mephibosheth, are you just going to wallow in your brokenness or accept that the Lord has got something in store for you?

As much as God understands, and the world understands, if you keep choosing your brokenness over your God-given seat at the king's table, it sets limitations to how far you can go. It is time to let it go because it has held you bound consistently. It is time to deal with it.

As long as you are still holding on to Lodebar, you can never move into Jerusalem. Lodebar will keep you subject to being treated like a servant. When you are in the king's palace, no one is looking at your legs, because all they see is a man with a royal garment on him and the favor of the king so, do not be afraid to walk in the palace. People cannot see the things you see, nor do they know the things you know so you do not need to tell them what they do not need to hear.

## *Chapter 5*

# THE REALITY OF TRANSITIONS

*This realization helped me make a smooth transition and maximize my growth opportunities.*

*Chapter 5*

# THE REALITY OF TRANSITIONS

Growing up in Benin City, Edo State, my parents were devout Catholics, and they did their best to carry my siblings and I us along with church activities. As the last child, the only option, then, was to follow my parents to church, but when I became a teenager, I started listening to sermons by Pastor Chris Oyakhilome from my elder sister. Gradually, I became deeply aware of God's presence, and it was then that I learned to communicate with Him in an expressive, personal, and intimate way. As a young girl, I found myself desiring to know more about God and asking Him to reveal Himself to me.

While at the university, I joined a fellowship and was always involved in one religious activity or the other. For us, "going to the mountain" was more than just fasting and praying. We visited real mountains to pray, held other meetings, and I became used to this path.

> *"True obedience is your humility to recognize the wisdom of God's word and turn to it"*

While my husband and I were engaged, I joined him at a church he was attending and it was a very different experience. They had an excellent selection of sound and lighting systems. The auditorium aesthetic did not match my mountain top experience. At that point, I was used to my style of fellowship, and it wasn't easy to adjust to anything else. I didn't feel at home during the service, but I couldn't run from it. I was on the journey of submitting to all things, and I didn't mind going to the same church as my husband- to-be.

> *"God utilizes the seasons of our lives, regardless of their origin, to prepare and position us to serve His purposes accurately and effectively"*

After we got married, we continued to attend church, and in my usual commitment to service, I gave everything I had. It wasn't long before I realized that there was more to the church than the packaging on Sundays. As I got involved in the prayer meetings, in-house planning, and other activities that helped me see things for what they actually were, I realized that their style of Service was only a sickle to attract people, but their passion and commitment to the ways of God and their love for people was unmatched. This realization helped me make a smooth transition and maximize my growth opportunities. At the age of 29, I was appointed a Resident Pastor of the church. I hope that doesn't sound like a motivational statement about growing your career, because I was not motivated when the assignment came.

The only thing I felt during that season was extreme anxiety. Despite being a young lady with little or no work or life experience, as Resident Pastor, I was expected to bring counsel and direction to people who I would ordinarily seek counsel and direction from.

Indeed, I can do anything through Christ, but that was the part where He strengthened me otherwise I would have made a mess of everything. At a point, I had to confide in my pastor to consider changing his mind, because I thought I was bound to fail and would rather excuse myself than disgrace him and the ministry. You would think this was my first exposure to leadership or that I was taking on new levels of responsibility, but that's not the case. The only explanation I have is in

Isaiah 60:1-2

*"Arise, shine, for your light has come, and the glory of the Lord rises upon you. See, darkness covers the earth and thick darkness is over the peoples, but the Lord rises upon you and his glory appears over you."*

There will come a time in your life when God will reset the order to which you have become accustomed. During this season, He will call you out of what you know, into what you barely understand at first. The call is to arise, but have you taken the time to ask why? Have you ever wondered why the call isn't for everyone? Why are you the only one going through your experiences? Why does everything seem to confound you?

Isaiah 60:2 (NIV):

*"See, darkness covers the earth and thick darkness is over the peoples, but the Lord rises upon you and his glory appears over you."*

The call to arise isn't because you are tired of sitting. You are not immune to the darkness that covers the earth and the gross darkness over the people. Left alone, you would rather be in charge and stick to the plan you've made for yourself, but God works differently. While everything seems normal and everyone is comfortable with the routine, He is doing something to you. He rises above you and His glory overshadows you. Don't be carried away with your idea of glory. The last time the glory of God overshadowed Mary, her integrity and marriage were threatened.

Luke 1:35 (NIV):

*"The angel answered, "The Holy Spirit will come upon you, and the power of the Highest will overshadow you."*

Matthew 1:19 (NIV):

*"Because Joseph, her husband, was faithful to the law, and yet did not want to expose her to public disgrace, he had in mind to divorce her quietly."*

The reason you have unique experiences is that God has highlighted you for what He is about to do, and He is calling you to your feet; to partner with Him to give birth to His will. Come to think of it, how else would you explain the story of Abraham in Genesis 12?

Genesis 11:31(NIV):

*"Terah took his son Abram, his grandson Lot, son of Haran, and his daughter-in-law Sarai, the wife of his son Abram, and together they set out from Ur of the Chaldeans to go to Canaan. But when they came to Harran, they settled there."*

Terah took the whole family on a journey to a defined destination—Canaan. In the course of the journey, they had a cause to settle in Harran. They got so comfortable in Harran, that they took on the identity of the land.

In Genesis 12:1, God asked Abram to leave: his country, his people, and his father's household.

Genesis 12:1

*"The Lord had said to Abram, 'Go from your country, your people, and your father's household to the land I will show you.'"*

When this instruction was given, it became clear that Terah had become too comfortable with Harran and forgot about the trip to Canaan. 'Comfort' doesn't necessarily mean laxity. It takes an element of success to build a household and be accepted into a foreign land. However, God can hold you back from your best moments, if it is not going to progress in His plan for your life. True obedience is your humility to recognize the wisdom of God's Word and turn to it. Before we continue, I must point out something; because the glory of the Lord singled you out and caused a shaking in your life doesn't mean you will receive an all- expense-paid offer to vacay in your chosen destination. After God asked Abraham to leave what He always knew how to do; leave his ideas of success and stability, with the assurance of making him a great nation and all the blessings of Genesis 12:2-3, you would expect God to lift him on the wings of the Eagle and bring him to his riches. After all, if "thou can prepare a table before me, in the presence of my enemies", what won't you do in their absence? In obedience to God—Jehovah Jireh (God Provider)—Abraham walked into a severe famine in a foreign nation and had to lean on a disguise and holy deception to survive. What happened to

> *"God can hold you back from your best moments, if it is not going to progress in His plan for your life"*

the great nation in Genesis 12:2?

If we compare experiences, Terah seemed to be more successful than Abraham: There was no record of having issues with settling down in Harran. He got to work and was able to raise a household there. However, in the case of Abraham, he had to resort to damage control to save his life and even risked losing his wife. The same situation, different experiences.

> *"It takes intimacy in fellowship with the holy spirit, to cultivate a heart that trusts in god, in his ways, and in his timing"*

Transitions often leave us unaware of what we are used to. Things you used to do without stress are now confusing you. Everything happens so fast, that even things we are familiar with, leaves us clutching onto the straws of our emotions.

While leading the church, I was constantly accused by the devil that my inexperience would lead to my failure and that I will disappoint the church leadership. In the following chapters of this book, I shared how God has helped me deal with imposter syndrome and the anxiety that accompanies this transition, but you must understand that the fragility of the process will set us up for our emotions to get the best of us.

The irony is that the transition comes in the form of horrible and heart-breaking experiences that leave you hurt and confused. Although they rarely look like anything better and more God-like, they contain tools to help you get through life.

We all go through transitions in our lives, and in different ways, but the ability to give meaning and voice to your experience is what makes it such a powerful tool in your hands. Your ability to evaluate your experiences through the lens of both God's Word and His plan is what empowers you for destiny.

To help you out, here are six (6) things to know about the transition:

**EVERY TRANSITION HAS A TIME-FRAME**

The fact is that there was a point when you didn't see anything wrong with your previous season, and even if you did, you couldn't have imagined the confusion that now overwhelms you in the name of a transition. However, there is a perspective I need you to be imparted with, as you go through the pages of this book, and it is that transitions are God's strategy to trigger the release of a promise. If you noticed, I didn't say they are God's rescue plan to avenge those who did you wrong in your previous season nor God's idea of punishing you for what you could have done differently. God had a purpose for which He initiated Creation, and you have a role to play in fulfilling that purpose in its entirety.

> *"When you least expect to move, God will move you"*

Accordingly, God always utilizes the seasons of our lives, regardless of their origin, to prepare and position us to serve His purposes accurately and effectively. It is this process of going through the seasons that causes you to birth His will in your life. This is what we call transitions. The truth about transitions that makes them uncomfortable is that they hit you without notice. When you least expect to move, God will move you, and your ability to handle that move will determine how you enter the new season.

After God helped me go through that phase of self-doubt, imposter syndrome, and anxiety (I outlined how it happened in the latter chapters of this book), I got to work. Although I still had a regular fight with fear in my room, when I started working, I worked and finished the job excellently, because God helped me. After the first year, I felt like I was made for the job. My entire life revolved around the ministry—my work and finances, my family, my mentors, my friends and associates, my co-workers, and so on. It was defined and fulfilling in itself; I had everything I needed in one place. What more could one pray for?

> *"To escape the process is to forfeit the promise."*

As months turned into years, as expected, I was applying pressure on the gas pedal, and God was helping me steer the wheel with the wisdom and guidance of mentors, and everything was going well.

In 2015, the Lord told me that I had completed my assignment in the ministry and it was time to move on.

In hindsight, I guess it would have been easier if He had made it clear that my service and Commitment to the Ministry was just for a season. At least, I would learn to count my days and put my heart in wisdom, as Moses said. Although that wasn't the case. It was a case of yesterday, everything was fine and in one place, today, God is asking me to leave behind; everything I have and everything I know. I couldn't imagine what the implications were, but I had to obey anyway.

It would be a great story if I said that I left everything I had and God provided abundantly, above all, the next day, but the truth is; the pain and the confusion that came with having to leave my job, my mentors, and mentees, my colleagues and all and disappear into thin air, numbed me for a while. I couldn't get myself together. I was almost lost in the pain, and all I remember was my sister asking me to 'give it five years.'

> *"God may be using your transition to bring you to a place of forgiveness"*

In her words, she said "Isi, in 5 years, even if you don't understand why it happened, you will appreciate what God did with it."

Although it looks like the last thing anyone in pain wants to hear, in 2020, I looked back and realized that it took me exactly 5 years to heal, when I had to make a transition that turned my life upside down. During those years, I tried many things in an attempt to make progress and put all of the confusion behind me, but the more I tried, the more I needed to try.

At some point, instead of running away from reality, I had to follow the process, trusting that God knew what He wanted to do with me and could see me through it all. Although God is using your transition to prepare you for the promise, it is up to you to decide whether to follow the process or seek a quick exit, but you must understand that to escape the process is to forfeit the promise.

The rigor of submitting to the process is often a result of our attachment to the pleasures or pain of the previous season. For God to truly work out His plan in your life, you must be willing to sacrifice the realities of your previous season on the altar of humility. Since every transition has a time frame, what you do during your transition matters a lot. Instead of being preoccupied with past pain or overwhelmed with uncertainty about what you're going through, here are three (3) things to do, while you wait.

> *"Clarity about what God is doing creates faith"*

**1. ASK FOR MERCY FOR THE THINGS THAT TRIGGERED THE TRANSITION**

As you go through transitions, there is a tendency to forget what triggered it in the first place. You need to intentionally identify your mistakes and what you could have done differently that brought you to this point. As you discover them, ask God to have mercy on you. Even if you have done nothing wrong, ask God to have mercy on the people and the system that has offended you. Ask God to have mercy on you and help you with your shortcomings. God may be using your transition to bring you to a place of forgiveness where you let go of those who have hurt you through no fault of your own.

## 2. SEPARATE FROM YOUR PLACES OF COMFORT

The moment of transition is not the time to insist on doing things your way or relying on your backup plan. You have to realize that if it is God who is bringing you into this season, then He has expectations of what He wants to do with you. Now is not the time to activate your 'relief system' to seek help. You must remain humble, depending on the Lord throughout this season. Spend time in fellowship with the Holy Spirit to cultivate a heart that trusts in God, in His ways, and His timing, and not a heart that is dependent on its understanding.

*". Be at peace with having to seek and follow God's pattern diligently,"*

## 3. PRAY FOR WISDOM AND CLARITY

The first thing you need, to come out of a transition is light- a revelation of the mind of God about your situation. Instead of spending time with people who would barely understand what you are going through, spend that time praying for wisdom and clarity. Clarity about what God is doing creates faith, which will keep you loyal to the process and the God of the process, no matter how long it takes.

It is possible to go through transitions in a shorter and easier period than you would ordinarily have because you can find and be humble to accept a prototype —someone who has gone through similar transitions accurately and obtained the promise—to model after. Notwithstanding the possibility of finding a prototype, don't be angry if you don't find one. Be at peace with having to seek and follow God's pattern diligently, no matter how unfamiliar it is to you and those who see you.

Refuse to be intimidated by onlookers into neglecting the glory of modelling a new path for others to follow.

## THE DRIVER OF TRANSITIONS

For you to make the most use out of what you're going through efficiently and accurately, you need to understand exactly what's going on, and I'll help you do that. It is pretty simple; God is bringing you into a new season, and the person you were doesn't fit into that season, so He had to subject you to a process, regardless of what brought you into it, to prepare you for His plan.

Since God has a plan and intercepts you in your comfort zone to bring you into that plan, what you do with that plan is up to you. Transitions aren't a one-way route to bliss and the fullness of the glory of God. At best, they depend on how much you can seek the mind of God and obey Him accordingly.

> *"He chose to do what was right which is defined by the proceeding Word —God's current perspective about the issue."*

As you go through the transition, you must understand that it is a process that requires you to submit. Regardless of the potential of a transition to cause transformation and birth the will of God in and through your life, if you are unwilling to submit to the ways of God despite your confusion and quest for quick fixes, you will arrive at a place away from God.

Luke 4:1-2:

*"Jesus, full of the Holy Spirit, left Jordan and was led by the Spirit into the wilderness, where for forty days he was tempted by the devil. He ate nothing during those days, and at the end of them, he was hungry."*

The Holy Spirit led Jesus into the wilderness to begin a transition. The dynamics of His transition required fasting and devotion to fellowship with the Father. As you reassess this story, you will realize that fasting is not a gift of the spirit, especially not for Jesus.

If you and I had to go into the wilderness, we would have had no choice but to fast, because there was no food, but for Jesus, even the devil knew that He could turn stones into bread if He wanted to. You may want to believe that the power to turn stones into bread is the result of fasting, but you need to understand that the devil spoke with conviction about what Jesus could do. Yet, He chose to stay hungry and submit to the government of God, living true to the requirements of His transition.

> *“. The wilderness might not be the ideal place for service, but it is the right place for pruning servants”*

His willingness to submit His will to the government of God during the transition made it easy to withstand the devil afterward. He didn't speak as one who was in lack and needed people to tell Him what to do, but as one who had trained His desires enough, by the Spirit, to be powered by God's opinion rather than His appetite. Against all traditions and religions which would have required Him to do what is good and obvious, He chose to do what was right which is defined by the proceeding Word—God's current perspective about the issue.

During your transition, you will be tempted by your ideas of what the solution to your experience is, but your ability to firmly believe in God's ways will maintain the integrity of your process. The goal is to put a knife to your throat and prune your appetite, for you to make decisions based on what God is saying rather than your quest for satisfaction, even when the satisfaction is the haste to get past the transition. You must decide to submit your will and desires to God, submitting to discover and obey whatever He instructs, at the instance of His word. In terms of your role in determining the outcome of the transition, there are three possibilities:

> *"Creation will submit to you only to the extent To which you submit to god's requirements for your life"*

**IF YOU DON'T SUBMIT TO GOD'S LEADING, YOU MAY GET STUCK OR EVEN BECOME A TOOL IN THE HANDS OF THE ENEMY**

Upon leaving Egypt in Exodus, the children of Israel got so blinded by the reality of freedom from slavery that they forgot why they had to be brought out of Egypt.

Exodus 5:1:

*"This is what the Lord, the God of Israel, says: 'Let my people go, so that they may hold a festival for me in the wilderness.'"*

God had specified that He would bring them out of Egypt to serve Him in the wilderness. Notice how He didn't talk about serving Him in the Promised Land? Have you ever wondered why? How you serve in the wilderness will determine whether or not you will reach the Promised Land. The wilderness might not be the ideal place for service, but it is the right place for pruning servants. It would seem that it was easier to serve God either in Egypt or Canaan than in the wilderness, because, in the wilderness, your progress is determined by two things:

a. Your ability to hear God's voice

b. Your attitude toward the last instruction you received.

As the children of Israel journeyed through the wilderness, from when God drowned the Egyptians, to when they made the golden calf, to how they responded to the acts of God, down to when Joshua sent spies to Jericho, one thing is obvious: they were a people who were bent on having things on their terms, regardless of how much God had proved Himself to them. Think of how their attitude of complaining about God's faithfulness manifested in His mighty works.

Psalm 95:10-11:

*"For forty years I was angry with that generation; I said, 'They are a people whose hearts go astray, and they have not known my ways.' So I declared an oath in my anger, They shall never enter my rest."*

Ask yourself these questions:

i. Did God bring them out of Egypt to destroy them?

ii. What did they do so badly that God couldn't ignore them?

iii. How come some people were saved from the destruction?

What did these people do differently?

If your answer is like mine, you will realize that the purpose of the wilderness, in how long we spend there and the conditions we are subjected to, is to prepare us for the Promise. While this is well- founded, it is our willingness to submit to the Lord's ways during the wilderness season that determines our outcome.

When we fail or delay in submission, we will wander in despair in the wilderness, realizing that the only way out is by the One who led us into it.

God speaks and gives you instructions on what to do in this season and how to do it, but it is left to you to obey or disregard it. In addition, you need to understand that the issue of obedience is more about how quickly you obey, rather than just obeying at any time you deem fit to. Remember, delayed obedience has repercussions to it. More than getting stuck in your wilderness season, you risk becoming a tool in the hands of the enemy and he will be empowered by your disobedience to afflict you.

> *"It is our willingness to submit to the Lord's ways during the wilderness season that determines our outcome"*

2. **IF YOU DON'T SUBMIT TO GOD'S LEADING, YOU WILL REMAIN PROUD AND VENGEFUL AGAINST GOD AND PEOPLE**

When you are not willing to submit to God's way, you might become filled with pride and anger from the memories of your previous season so much that you become vengeful.

Numbers 11:5 (NIV):

*"We remember the fish we ate in Egypt at no cost— also the cucumbers, melons, leeks, onions, and garlic."*

Just as the children of Israel preferred onions and garlic to God's providence, you will eventually express your disappointment to God when you insist on wanting Him to do everything your way. The enemy will take advantage of your pride and anger to validate your actions and trap you in them. You will be filled with pride in how much better you deserve and can get for yourself at will. You begin to degrade God and those around you to the point where the outcome of your transition will be worse than when you started. You might be tempted to believe that you are in charge, but you need to realize that when you have a strong desire to assert your self-worth and blame others for everything, God is unlikely to be there. The enemy has hijacked your pain and is manipulating you out of the will of God.

*"Most times, we don't realize how much we have been stuck in the usual until God begins to call us into a newness"*

The way of God is the way of forgiveness, humility, submission, and progress. However, it goes beyond presenting your weaknesses to God. You need to humbly present your strong reasons why you deserve better. You aren't presenting it because you want God to validate you and show everybody that you were right after all, and you truly deserved better, but you do so because you know that God knows better. You know that although forgiveness might look like weakness, it is strength indeed, and when humility looks frail, the strength of the Spirit is made perfect in your life.

## 2 SUBMITTING TO GOD COULD BE SHAMEFUL

As I said, it is easier to submit when you are wrong. It is a symptom of chronic foolishness to boast about your mistakes. The reality of having to let go and let God, even when it feels like you know exactly what you need to do and how to come out of your transition as quickly as possible, might be shameful. You could put a call through to a few people and make arrangements for you to get into a new place immediately, but God might be asking you to wait.

There are times when it takes faith to wait, especially when you are not ignorant of the steps you should take, but instead, choose to wait for the steps God wants you to take. You may have an idea of what God should do to the people and systems you are coming from and where next He should take you, but you need to understand that God is not in the business of validating your desires. God is more concerned about the transformation that prepares you for His desire for you.

> *"It is a symptom of chronic foolishness to boast about your mistakes"*

The dynamics of transformation that comes with transition lie in your ability to:

- Believe that God sees and understands your pain and aspirations.

- Believe that God has a more sustainable pathway to where He is leading you to.
- Let go of your plans in submission to God's plan.
- Be humble enough to not let the memory of your plan interrupt your submission when the going gets tough.

As you submit to God's way, regardless of how much hurt you feel, you become progressively more loving and kind, and you find confidence in your vulnerability. The real purpose of submission is not only to provide you with succour and a coping mechanism but also to teach you the way of the Spirit in obedience. Your transition raises questions about your life that God wants to help you address. As your Creator, He knows your tendencies and how much they can short-change His plan for you if you let them have their way. The Lord then attempts to make you perfect by calling you to step out of what you would ordinarily do and submit to what He is calling you to do. The graphic picture of submission was painted by Paul in 2 Corinthians 4:16-17 and expressed by Jesus on the Cross.

> *"There are times when it takes faith to wait"*

*2 Corinthians 4:16 -17:*

*"Therefore, we do not lose heart. Though outwardly we are wasting away, inwardly we are being renewed day by day. For our light and momentary troubles are achieving for us an eternal glory that far outweighs them all,"*

It seems that since Jesus was destined to be crucified from birth (scriptures even say He was slain from the foundation of the world), He would have a red-carpet reception to the cross with a cup of smoothie in His hand. Don't get carried away with the drama in Psalms 24:7-10 that you miss the message.

*"Lift up your heads, you gates; be lifted, you ancient doors, that the King of glory may come in. Who is this King of glory? The Lord is strong and mighty, the Lord is mighty in battle. Lift up your heads, you gates; lift them, you ancient doors that the King of glory may come in. Who is he, this King of glory? The Lord Almighty—He is the King of glory"*

The gates are only lifted at the Lord's command, and Jesus could only access this reality through His surrender on the cross; the pain, shame, and ridicule of the cross included. It is easy to forget about the ridicule that came with having to publicly shame a man whom, hours earlier, was the joy of the whole nation, but it is in His submission to the bits and pieces, the ridicule of having to be exchanged for a thief and dying the death assigned to one who God called 'cursed.' (Galatians 3:13 "Cursed is everyone who is hung on a pole.") It is in all of these that He received a name that is above every other name.

> *"God is more concerned about the transformation that prepares you for His desire for you."*

Jesus' manifestation in Psalm 24 is not a case of eloquence or poise. Creation will submit to you only to the extent to which you submit to God's requirements for your life. The reality of letting go and letting God will not be easy, because you have to deny yourself and accept the weight of God's ways.

In all of this, the joy remains that the glory of our submission is made perfect in the suffering we endure for righteousness' sake. When we surrender to God in times of confusion, we make more room for the Spirit to dwell in us. In Isaiah 11:2-5, we see the picture of a man in whom the Spirit dwells lavishly.

*"The Spirit of the Lord will rest on him—the Spirit of wisdom and understanding, the Spirit of counsel and might, the Spirit of the knowledge and fear of the Lord—and he will delight in the fear of the Lord. He will not judge by what he sees with his eyes, or decide by what he hears with his ears; but with righteousness, he will judge the needy, with justice he will give decisions for the poor of the earth. He will strike the earth with the rod of his mouth; with the breath of his lips, he will slay the wicked. Righteousness will be his belt and faithfulness the sash around his waist."*

We see that the result of the indwelling of the Spirit is not mere charisma. But the ability to discern the Spirit from the flesh. Over time, after training your senses to submit to God's wisdom in all situations, wilfully yielding to God's ways, your perception will go beyond what you are used to, to evaluating life by God's standard.

You will become a model of what God would do per time, by how much space you give the Holy Spirit to manifest His will through your vessel so that men could see Him. God would even ask men to look at you for direction, knowing that your loyalty is to do the will of God and to please Him.

By submitting to the works of God in your life, you are positioning yourself, by the Spirit, to be given new levels of responsibility, based on your ability to follow directions.

## THE CALL TO CHANGE

As you discern and submit to God's will for your transition, you will have a reason to step outside of what you are used to and meet the demands of the new season. As you make progress, your plan will be fully adjusted or revised, and you must be willing to accept these changes, and to accelerate your transition. You are not always the one to regulate what you always know.

> *"Refuse to be gas lighted or blackmailed into sharing what God is doing in your life with people who have no role to play in the outcome of your transition"*

Sometimes, we don't realize how much we have been stuck in the usual and that God is calling us to take a leap of faith into uncertainty. The only confidence you will ever have is that God, who asked you, will be with you throughout the process and on the other side of the leap, waiting for you.

During your transition, you will have to get used to taking risks. The challenge most people face is not that transitions change everything around them, but that they are forced to change from what they have always been. This alone paralyzes most people and causes them to find a way out of the pruning of the transitions, and, as we have seen, they will eventually drift away from God's Promise. The case is very simple. Either you dedicate yourself to the pursuit of the promise or you take the route of convenience. Only that true convenience is one of the fruits of the Promise.

As you make changes during your transition, you must be aware of people who relate with you merely because of what you are and what you have. Expect them to leave when you are no longer what they used to know. Don't fight or be worried about it. It is all a part of the pruning process and you have to get comfortable with it.

Like in the case of Naomi and Ruth, God might cause a transition to get you out of the environment you are used to, and to where He has proposed to bring you into the fullness of His plan. God's call for Ruth to leave Moab was an attempt to position her for destiny.

In Moab, only God knew the fate of a young widow. Instead of letting her wallow in Moab, even where wallow could mean a level of success, He brought her into a system with prepared laws to accommodate her experience and prepare her for the Promise. It seems that Boaz was doing her a favor by marrying her, but you have to realize that he was subject to a law that governed Israel - a law that requires whoever acquired the property of his deceased kinsman to marry his widow to raise seed for his kinsman. This was part of the laws given to Moses in Deuteronomy 25:5-9, and who would have thought that it would result in the birth of King David's grandfather? The law and Boaz could have remained in Bethlehem forever, if Ruth stayed back in Moab.

> *"Creation will submit to you only to the extent to which you submit to God's requirements for your life"*

Your ability to discern the next move of God in a location different from where you are, and your humility to move at the instance of the revelation, is what delivers the promise to you. That location could be where God has prepared laws, people, and systems to give you an advantage because of what you have been through, and not necessarily despite it. It might not mean having to leave your physical location. It could be your relationships, your job, or any other environment you are used to. God might be sending you to a place where your scars will be what qualifies you for the promise, but you must be willing to move.

> *"The strength of faith that comes from your fellowship with the Holy Spirit will preserve you against the lies and accusations of the enemy"*

## CHANGE OF PERSPECTIVE

Esther 4:11-16:

*"All the king's officials and the people of the royal provinces know that for any man or woman who approaches the king in the inner court without being summoned, the king has but one law: that they are put to death unless the king extends the gold scepter to them and spares their lives. But thirty days have passed since I was called to go to the king." When Esther's words were reported to Mordecai, he sent back this answer: 'Do not think that because you are in the king's house you alone of all the Jews will escape. For if you remain silent at this time, relief and deliverance for the Jews will arise from another place, but you and your father's family will perish. And who knows but that you have come to your royal position for such a time as this?' Then Esther sent this reply to Mordecai: "Go, gather together all the Jews who are in Susa, and fast for me. Do not eat or drink for three days, night or day. I and my attendants will fast as you do. When this is done, I will go to the king, even though it is against the law. And if I*

*perish, I perish."*

The goal of the changes you experience during this season is expected to change how you evaluate life. The result of your transformation is that you can see and evaluate things from God's point of view, relying on His justice and power, despite all the difficulties. Most times, we get carried away by the realities of our current season - pain and pleasure alike-that we are quick to give reasons why the change we are being called to make might not be possible. _This was the story of Queen Esther. When the King had a cause to replace Queen Vashti, her cousin Mordecai used his access to the palace to draft her into the group of women to be selected, handing her over to Haggai, the one in charge of the women.

During and even after becoming queen, Mordecai made it clear to Esther that she needed to conceal her nationality and background to avoid unnecessary attention. It was easy for the reality of her background to become dormant once she became Queen. She had privileges her nationality could not afford and favor with people her kinsmen could only dream of. She became used to the culture of the palace so much that when Mordecai revealed Haman's plot against the Jews, she was quick to cite palace protocol as why the task seemed impossible.

When did Esther start trusting the system more than Mordecai? How could she forget that her true identity was a secret Haman could exploit for her execution, if he knew? You cannot blame her. That is one of the things that come with being in a system that works—you can barely think of going against it.

When Mordecai was positioning her to be queen, all he had in mind was seeking the best for his orphaned cousin. At this point, he realized the relevance of what God did in making her queen, and how her reasons, though valid, threatened God's plan. It was up to Mordecai to admonish her or get frustrated by her excuses.

Mordecai himself was living in tandem with God's agenda for keeping him around the palace, which was to obtain first-hand information and act accordingly from a place of strength. He had owned up to the responsibility that was assigned him and he made it clear to Esther that if she chose to shy away from *her own* responsibility at that point, God was going to send salvation from elsewhere, and she would be consumed by her secret. The message was all it took for Esther to understand the true nature of the setup she found herself in. That is what transitions do to you. They allow you to see things through God's eyes.

> *"True convenience is one of the fruits of the Promise"*

Since you will have to act in certain ways to properly handle your transition, your actions are determined by how you assess the situation. If you don't have an accurate perspective on the issue, your efforts to navigate through will not lead to the promise. You need to be humble enough to accept that your view of the situation may not be the whole truth, and your readiness to submit to a more accurate perspective will help you triumphantly engage the current season.

**THE BURDEN OF RESPONSIBILITY**

The reality of transitions lies in the impact they have on your life. They often leave you desperate and confused, especially when it comes to how suddenly they happen. When we're going through a transition, we tend to be so preoccupied trying to understand what we're going through so much that we end up making it all about us. Although it looks like you are the only one affected by the rapid changes taking place, you must accept that others are connected to you. You need to understand that anything that affects you deeply enough to make you leave where you are will also affect them because they will feel discouraged if they are unable to find you. Sure, you're responsible for the outcome of your transition, but how you manage your relationships also contributes to the fate of your transition.

> *"Your humility to move at the instance of the revelation, is what delivers the promise to you"*

Your preoccupation with finding a way out doesn't negate your responsibility to those to whom you are accountable. The first thing to do during a transition is to understand what is going on. You may not understand why it happened or what triggered it, but at least you need to know what is going on, especially how you feel.

When you clearly understand what you are going through, you will be able to communicate better with those for whom you are responsible. You need to help them understand the current reality, the changes that have occurred, what your posture and response are, and what you expect of them. Your inability to make them understand what you are going through will leave them feeling lost and abandoned, which is something no one should feel in a relationship, especially when they didn't do anything wrong.

> *"The goal of the changes you experience during this season is expected to change how you evaluate life"*

Those who are accountable to you make it their responsibility to assist you to go through life, trying to ease your burdens in their little way, and where they don't even understand what your burdens are, how can they assist you effectively, if they can at all? Don't be pressured by your emotions to believe that you have to do it alone, and as such you don't have to tell anybody about what is going on.

This sounds reasonable, but you have to realize that the only way the enemy can attack you is to pull you away from where you have strength and support and where you have people who can defend and cater to you while you fight, into a place where you have to confront life alone. Think of Jesus and His journey to the cross.

Matthew 26:37-38:

*"He took Peter and the two sons of Zebedee along with him, and he began to be sorrowful and troubled. Then he said to them, 'My soul is overwhelmed with sorrow to the point of death. Stay here and keep watch with me.'"*

As sacred and singular as His journey was, He didn't keep it to Himself. Even when He spoke to the crowd in parables, He was vulnerable enough to share His burden with Peter, James, and John, not because they had the power to ease his burden, but because in enduring the process with Him, their own convictions in Him and what it was that He was calling them to do would be reinforced.

The weight of transition is often hard to bear, to the point where you get so caught up in trying to find stability in the midst of all the disillusionment that you forget to carry those in your life along. During this time, sharing your experiences might feel like a burden, either because you are trying to focus on solving the problem or you just wouldn't want to disturb others with your problem. *"After all, everybody has got a fair share of problems to keep them busy. Why should I bother others with mine?"* You might ask.

> *"If you don't have an accurate perspective on the issue, your efforts to navigate through will not lead to the promise"*

In all of this, it takes having a mature sense of responsibility and accountability to identify those who are or will be affected by the changes in your life and to communicate your experiences enough for them to understand what you are going through and find ways to assist you where they can.

On the contrary, you must be discerning to know to whom you are accountable. Refuse to be gas lighted or blackmailed into sharing what God is doing in your life with people who have no role to play in the outcome of your transition.

## THE PLACE OF ENCOUNTERS

Once you have a clear understanding of what you are going through, remember that the ultimate goal of the transition is to make you a gate through which others can access a dimension of God. God is birthing a model in you by which others will find the wisdom of God to accurately steward their transitions. It matters how your fellowship has been. If your fellowship depends on where you are or what you have, it will be hard for you to find God when these things are taken away from you in your transition.

It will take true communion with the Spirit, where your sole focus is on seeking Christ and doing His will, to access God's mind about your present times, and discover how He wants you to handle it. When you are in communion with the Word, prayer, and worship, you are brought into the accurate perspective of Christ and His eternal purpose, and the impartation of grace that comes with having to understand what God is set to achieve through what is happening will be your peace. The strength of faith that comes from your communion will preserve you against the lies and accusations of the enemy.

> *"The reality of transitions lies in the impact they have on your life"*

When you weigh the realities of living for Christ against having to be affected by how people treat you and your need to defend yourself, you will realize that trying to prove a point or hold on to offense is futile. At that juncture, what comes or does not, what stays or does not is of little relevance.

It doesn't matter what comes or doesn't, what stays or goes. What matters is your commitment to serve Jesus and do your best to participate in the fulfilment of His will, no matter what you may have to go through.

Furthermore, you shouldn't be in a hurry to bully God with your demands to know what He is doing or where He is taking you to. You might relinquish the promise if you don't handle the unscriptural expectations you have of God, especially the ones that make you believe that God is a genie that grants your random wishes. You have to be content with the fact that even if God does not categorically reveal to you what's next, He will give you the grace to be effective in the current season.

> *"Your preoccupation with finding a way out doesn't negate your responsibility to those to whom you are accountable"*

In David's experience of fleeing Saul, he learned to find solace in fellowship with God, so much so that he was governed by God's presence, even when others believed that he had the right to act on the contrary. As a man whose heart longed for God's perfection, he was able to go beyond God's perspective about his condition to the point where God could reveal His agenda for humanity to David.

It was through the power of his encounters that he could look beyond his predicament to devote himself to what was available, even when beggars themselves come to him for refuge. David did not seek to raise mighty men. He was only faithful to what he had, to the point of blessing everyone during his transition. The success of your transition makes you a model to others. They will discover God's blueprint for handling their challenge by just looking at you. With this as a reminder of what you're supposed to show others, you have to survive and grow during your transition season.

> *"Don't be pressured by your emotions to believe that you have to do it alone"*

**SURVIVAL VS GROWTH**

My mother was an Officer in the Nigeria Police force, and as her youngest child, I was her 'handbag'. Whenever she was transferred to a new station, often away from home, I followed suit. In the course of following her around several transfers, I attended fourteen schools. I know you are astonished by the number, but this goes beyond that. As a child, all I knew was that, for every new transfer, there was a corresponding change in environment, school, neighbors, and friends.

God used the reminiscence of that significant aspect of my childhood to show me how much having to go through these incessant transitions in quick succession affected me. Because I had to adjust to a new environment every time my mother was transferred, I unconsciously had to do away with my history; my previous school, friends, and neighbors, as soon as I arrived.

Although I am a typical introvert who would prefer to stay in her space, I found myself adjusting my personality to suit my circumstances. Despite having to devise ways to live in the moment, without recourse to the past or future, I couldn't commit to anything at all. Why would I, when a letter from the Police would leave me no option but to let go of everything and everyone? I grew to believe that no one was too important to not be forgotten, hence I not only learned to numb the pain that comes with letting go, but I was also quick to walk away from anything that demanded much from me. I was all for survival; how to enjoy or run away from this phase while it lasts, indifferent about the future and what it held. If you will be honest, you can relate to my experience.

> *"Because the fact that they went through the process with Him will reinforce their conviction in Him and what He was calling them to do"*

As you go through seasons in your life, pleasure and pain alike, you are often distracted from the big picture. You are carried away by coping with what is left, trying to not delve into uncertainty again. When Abraham set out on the journey to obey God, he got to the Negev in Genesis 12:9 where he had such a terrible experience with the famine and drought in the land that he considered taking refuge in Egypt. After developing an airtight cover-up strategy, he got to Egypt in search of survival. While he had to trade his wife for his safety, he was also favored accordingly.

From what began as a search for survival, it got to a point where Sarah, Abraham's wife, was living with the Pharaoh as though married to him, while Abraham was busy acquiring wealth and possessions.

Genesis 12:16-17:

*"He treated Abram well for her sake, and Abram acquired sheep and cattle, male and female donkeys, male and female servants, and camels. But the Lord inflicted serious diseases on Pharaoh and his household because of Abram's wife Sarai."*

It is easy to find so much comfort in survival that you sacrifice the journey ahead. It took divine intervention for Abraham to let go of survival in search of destiny. As you go through the different seasons of your life, you must learn to leverage them as opportunities for growth. See everything as a tool for your advancement, regardless of the condition. Instead of letting your emotions take over, allow yourself to learn from your experience.

> *"The ultimate goal of the transition is to make you a gate through which others can access a dimension of God"*

## *Chapter 6*

# REEVALUATING YOUR TRANSITIONS

*Your ability to understand what you are going through and give voice to it makes it a powerful tool in your hands.*

# Chapter 6

# REEVALUATING YOUR TRANSITIONS

The intent of a transition isn't just to expose you to harsh times but to prepare you and get you to a place where you can manifest the promise.

Your ability to ask the right questions will determine how quickly you will come out of it. Not only should you identify where you are coming from, where you are, and where you are going, you also need to understand how they relate and how to navigate through the past and present to arrive at the promise.

As I said, your ability to understand what you are going through and give voice to it makes it a powerful tool in your hands, but because transitions are emotionally driven, people usually have difficulty asking questions, let alone seeing what's in front of them. In this chapter, I have put together nine (9) questions you need to answer, to help understand what you're going through and provide a roadmap on how to emerge from it.

> *"All that is of God seeks to edify you and position you to accurately reflect God's will"*

## 1. WHAT AM I FEELING?

Transitions are not a time to leave anything to chance so do not attempt to simply ignore your feelings. You may be overwhelmed by feelings of shame, pain, loneliness, and confusion, and your insecurities may cause the door of courage to be attacked. In the thick of the storm brewing within you, you need to pinpoint exactly what you're feeling, not just how. 'I feel bad' or 'I feel vulnerable' is not enough.

Be specific with the emotions you feel and the kingdom that those emotions represent. Do you feel betrayed? Are you afraid of uncertainty? Are you nostalgic from the last season? Your ability to recognize and understand the emotions that govern your transition will help you distinguish sacred emotions from demonic emotions. You may be wondering how to distinguish the two, but don't worry, I'll help you.

> *"Sustain the discernment to know those who God has prepared to journey with you to the other side"*

Godly emotions seek forgiveness, restoration, and righteousness, despite the pain seeking to obscure them, while demonic emotions preoccupy you with thoughts of pain, revenge and unforgiveness making you neglect what God is doing. You must understand that all that is of God seeks to edify you and position you to accurately reflect God's will. Anything that fails to do so should be tested by God's Word and prayers. The bald truth is that your emotions will drive you to make decisions and your decisions determine how you get through this season. The sooner you deal with your feelings, the more time you have to focus on managing your current season.

## 2 HOW IS THIS PROCESS AFFECTING MY PERSONALITY?

During the transition, you need to be prepared for the changes that will happen. Once you understand what is going on, you need to understand how that process affects your personality as an individual. Transitions are designed to align you with God's agenda, and changes in your personality must also reflect this Truth.

> *"Don't be afraid to hold onto those who God asks you to stand with, no matter how others feel neglected"*

As you make progress in your transition, you will find people who will persist in talking about how much you've changed, but your understanding of the transition's impact on your personality will bring you peace and direction for complaints. The failure to grasp this will see you victimized by a terrible spiritual transaction where you trade the goal of God for the good of men, because you were unable to withstand the complaints of close associates, who had little understanding of your need to change.

## 3 WHO WOULD GOD HAVE ME SHARE THIS SEASON WITH?

While it is impossible to overemphasize how relevant relationships are in navigating through transitions, the success of your transitions is highly related to the quality of your association. Any attempt to trivialize your transition by not treating it with the sensitivity it deserves, usually by sharing your experiences without discretion, will ultimately affect the whole process. You need to identify specific people with whom God wants you to share your experiences.

*Matthew 26:37-38:*

*"He took Peter and the two sons of Zebedee along with him, and he began to be sorrowful and troubled. Then he said to them, 'My soul is overwhelmed with sorrow to the point of death. Stay here and keep watch with me.'"*

> *"The most important source of peace, stability and direction in transition is a clear sense of purpose"*

Like Jesus, even among your 12, you will have to identify your Peter, James, and John—people who will follow you to the cross and tarry there, despite their human weaknesses. As you communicate with the crowd in parables, you must sustain the discernment to know those who God has prepared to journey with you to the other side. If we judge how Jesus chooses His inner circle — *"The Three"*—based on fairness, it would look like He was showing favoritism or giving preferential treatment to those He liked. From another angle, have you considered that, after all was said and done, it was 'The Three' who formed the foundation upon which the church thrives? By discernment, Jesus saw that these men were worth the investment of His experiences; pain, encounters, and pleasure alike, seeing that they would remain committed to Him, even after all was said and done. This should be an effective guide on how you relate with people during transitions.

In addition to discerning whom to share His transitions with, due to the weightiness of transitions, Jesus was able to identify Judas and his plot. During transitions, your level of awareness and instinctiveness heightens, to the point where your mind identifies and helps you deal with things that you would ordinarily not agree to.

Do not be afraid to hold onto those who God asks you to stand with, no matter how neglected others feel.

> *"Your understanding of your destination determines the means and companions you will take with you"*

Accept the burden of responsibility by all means, however there is more to transitions than making everyone try to understand what you are going through.

## 4. WHERE AM I GOING?

The most important source of peace, stability and direction in transition is a clear sense of purpose. If you know where God is taking you, you won't spend time with people and places that won't get you there.

Transition is not the time to seek temporary relief or a facade of comfort. True comfort is in living in the fullness of God's will at all times, and until you do, everything else is a distraction. The ultimate perspective on transitions is in the outcome.

It is good to understand where you are coming from, why you had to leave, and where you are presently, but if you don't understand where God is taking you, how will you know what would take you there or know when you arrive?

The understanding of your destination determines the means and companions you will take with you. It will define your appearance, your posture, and how you prepare. Sit back and find out where God is leading you this season. A clear sense of purpose will guide you to invest your resources into things that are consistent with God's plan for that season. Even when you are trying to figure out where God is taking you, spend time preparing for a banquet with kings.

> *"Anything you don't understand and deal with will always bring you back to where you started"*

### 5. WHY DID I HAVE TO LEAVE THERE?

There is always the pain and confusion of having to leave the previous season, and the hurry to get into the new season. However, anything you don't understand and deal with will always bring you back to where you started.

Understanding why you had to leave your previous season doesn't necessarily mean that you have to judge or condemn it. We're trying to figure out what in the new season keeps you from continuing where you left off.

What is God trying to accomplish through you that He has to bring you out of where you were before? The quality of the answers you find to this question will bring peace and make you content with where you are, whatever it may seem like, knowing that God has a reason to call you out from it.

> *"God was so confident in Job's ability to manage, that He wanted to show the devil what Job would do with suffering"*

## 6. HOW DO I STEWARD MY CURRENT SEASON?

The story that comes to mind is Job's confession in Job 13:15 "Though he slays me, yet will I hope in him; I will surely defend my ways to his face." It is so easy to identify Job as the perfect picture of suffering and the frailty of our humanity, so much so that we don't recognize that what mattered most was his Stewardship. God was so confident in Job's ability to manage, that He wanted to show the devil what Job would do with suffering. His confession in Job 13:15 says it all.

To effectively steward this season, you must know these three things:

- Be assured that if God brings you into a time of abundance and leads you through a time of despair, it is all an effort to do His good in you. While that doesn't mean that God is responsible for the unattractive experiences you go through, His reality as Father makes Him use everything, we go through to serve us His eternal plan. This perspective helps you both understand and maximize the seasons you're going through.

- You must be sensitive to the songs, the instructions, and the scriptures He keeps repeating, as you go through this season. As you receive these signals and messages from the Spirit, be sure to document them. Take a record of everything that God does during this season.
- Pray through everything in this season. Ask the Spirit for direction.

As you cultivate these three things in this season, the Spirit of God will lead you into the perfect will of God.

## 7. WHAT DOES GOD WANT ME TO LEARN?

The sensitivity of transitions allows different sources to try to explain what you are going through. You're often bombarded by people's opinions on what brought you here and what you should do, but it is up to you to figure out what right lessons you expect to learn from this season.

> *"To understand what you are going through, you need to understand your role in it"*

History is replete with people who have been left bitter, hateful, malicious, selfish, and greedy because they chose to pay attention to the wrong lessons from their transition. You need to partner with the Holy Spirit to know what God is showing you through this experience.

Could it be that He needs you to learn how to be confident and speak up when it matters? Maybe he needs you to learn to be confident and speak up when there's a problem. It can also teach you better ways to interact with people or manage your resources—people and gifts. Transitions aren't the time to give room to doctrines of men and demons. You must focus your energy on things that give life and bring you closer to the Spirit.

## 8. WHY AM I CAUGHT IN THIS PROCESS?

It is possible to get stuck while trying to hurry out of transitions that you fail to ask yourself why you are still there. Why does time seem to stand still, as though God doesn't care what you're going through? Is there something you need to learn, someone you need to meet, or somewhere you need to go? Your answer to this question will help you glean accurate lessons from the season.

Your willingness to accept that it is God who has allowed you to be there for this long determines how you learn and maximize the lessons of where you are, which will lead you to where you need to be. Truth is indeed liberating, but until you enter into the fullness of truth (God's strategy for dealing with the season you are in), that reality of freedom is still ahead of you.

## 9. HOW DID THIS ALL HAPPEN?

After Pharaoh's daughter adopted Moses, although he enjoyed the privileges of the royal family of Egypt, his heart remained fixed on the fate of his people, the Israelites.

*Exodus 2:11-12:*

*"One day, after Moses had grown up, he went out to where his people were and watched them at their hard labor. He saw an Egyptian beating a Hebrew, one of his people. Looking this way and that and seeing no one, he killed the Egyptian and hid him in the sand."*

Since you might want to justify his killing of the Egyptian, his decision to flee from Egypt proves that he knew he had made a mistake, else, since he wasn't a stranger to the palace, he would have insisted on making his case and defending his actions.

Without a doubt, God called him to free Israel. It is clear that the appointed time for him to learn God's ways was near, and God must bring him out of Egypt, but because God uses our shortcomings as a tool to engineer His will, that doesn't mean He validates our mistakes. Moses, although in a transition, realized that what led to his departure from Egypt was his fault.

It could not be further from the truth to think that the reason Moses debated with God about who would rescue Israel from Egypt, especially about going up to Pharaoh, is not related to why he left Egypt in the first place.

In today's world, it would have been easier to blame Pharaoh for witch-hunting or accuse him of being wicked, rather than point out the fact that Moses wasn't innocent, and that Pharaoh had the right to enforce law and order in his kingdom.

As you go through transitions, you must identify what you could have done differently. Don't get so carried away by the pain that you believe you did nothing wrong, and that you are only a victim of the limitations of where you are coming from. To understand what you are going through, you need to understand your role in it.

It was the Word of God and his encounter with Jehovah that gave Moses the grace to confront the system he once shunned, and that was only possible because instead of playing the blame game, he realized that he had scores to settle in Egypt. While this is a call to accept responsibility for the things you can do better, it is also a call to celebrate the things you did well last season. The idea is not to create complacency, but to clarify your strengths and limitations, and point out to you the areas you need to improve on in your transition. Your ability to improve in these areas positions you advantageously for the new season.

## *Chapter 7*

# LEVERAGING AND MANAGING RELATIONSHIPS

*This can include friends and family members who can offer a listening ear and a shoulder to lean on when things get tough.*

*Chapter 7*

# LEVERAGING AND MANAGING RELATIONSHIPS

Leveraging relationships is an important factor in making successful transitions. Relationships provide us with the support, guidance, and connections that are often necessary for navigating new situations and environments. When going through a transition, it is important to identify and leverage the relationships that can be most helpful.

First, relationships can provide emotional support during times of change. This can include friends and family members who can offer a listening ear and a shoulder to lean on when things get tough. Feeling supported can help us manage stress, build resilience, and stay focused on our goals and aspirations.

> "Be intentional and proactive"

Second, relationships can provide guidance and advice based on their own experiences. This can include colleagues, mentors, and other professionals who can offer insights and perspectives on how to navigate the challenges and opportunities of the transition. They may be able to provide tips on how to network, find job opportunities, or overcome. In addition to these things, relationships can also provide us with connections to new opportunities and resources. This can include introductions to people in our new community or industry, or recommendations for new job opportunities. These connections can help us more quickly and easily adjust to our new situation, and can open up new possibilities for growth and development.

> *“When you are spending all you have to stay afloat, you will have to rely on the value of the contribution your closest relationships have to offer”*

In order to leverage relationships successfully during a transition, it is important to be intentional and proactive. This means identifying the relationships that will be most helpful, and taking steps to build and nurture those relationships.

It is easy to guard yourself when you are stable and have a good grasp of what is going on in your life, but when you are spending all you have to stay afloat, you will have to rely on the value of the contributions your closest relationships have to offer.

As with everything in life, there are also different types of people you will meet during your transition, but what matters is what you can make out of it and how each relationship affects your fate. During your transition, you will discover the power of relationships, and how they can make or break what God is doing with you. Some of the people in your life during the time of your transition are your burden bearers. They are vessels that God uses to help you navigate that season of your life.

**BURDEN BEARERS**

Burden bearers can play a crucial role in making successful transitions. These are individuals who are willing and able to provide support, guidance, and encouragement during times of change and transition. Having burden bearers can help individuals navigate the challenges and uncertainties of transitions.

They can provide emotional support, offer practical advice, and serve as a sounding board for ideas and concerns. They can also offer insights and perspectives that may not have been considered, and provide a sense of accountability and motivation to stay on track.

Burden bearers can provide a number of different types of support. For example, they can be good listeners who provide a safe and non-judgmental space for us to express our fears, doubts, and concerns. They can also offer words of encouragement and affirmation, reminding us of our strengths and abilities when we are feeling low.

> *"In our quest for ease and favors, we get so occupied with this that we fail to realize that there is more to favor than hand-outs"*

Burden bearers can come in many forms, including family members, friends, colleagues, mentors, coaches, and therapists. The key is to identify individuals who are supportive, trustworthy, and have experience or expertise relevant to the transition.

By having burden bearers, individuals can feel more confident and supported as they navigate transitions. They can also benefit from the insights, perspectives, and guidance provided by others, which can help them make better decisions and take effective actions toward their goals and aspirations.

> *"The fastest way to be replenished is to feast on the word from those who can rightly divide truth into pieces that nourish you with the life of God "*

We are all used to praying for 'destiny helpers' —people who will lavishly support us with their skills unconditionally, even when we don't merit support. In our quest for ease and favors, we get so occupied with this that we fail to realize that there is more to favor than hand-outs. People who receive favors don't measure it by what they get, but by the loyalty and dedication people have for them and their vision.

In transitions, one category of destiny helper you need is burden bearers - those who will stick their neck out to see to your peace, joy, stability, and progress. I have outlined five kinds of burden bearers you will need for a successful transition. They include the following;

## 1. A TRUSTED, COMPETENT PRIEST

During times of transition, you may be grappling with questions of meaning, purpose, and identity, and a priest can provide guidance on how to navigate these issues from a spiritual perspective. This can involve exploring questions of faith, discussing how to maintain a sense of purpose during times of change, and helping to discern what God may be calling us to in this new season of life.

In addition to that, a priest can offer pastoral care and support. During times of transition, you may be dealing with a range of emotions, from fear and uncertainty to grief and loss. A priest can provide a compassionate and non- judgmental listening ear, offering support and encouragement as you navigate the challenges of the transition process.

> “*It is the truth that makes you free, not what your ears are itching for. Don't let your insecurities cheat you*”

Additionally, a priest can help you to connect with others in our community who may be able to offer additional support and resources.

Finally, a priest can help you to connect with the broader church community. Transitions can be isolating, but a priest can help people to stay connected to the larger community of faith. This might involve connecting you with a small group or Bible study, helping them find a ministry to serve in, or simply encouraging them to attend worship services and other church events.

The trust element is crucial when it comes to seeking the guidance of a priest during a time of transition because it allows for an open and honest relationship to develop. People who are going through major life changes are often feeling vulnerable, uncertain, and maybe even disillusioned. Therefore, it is essential for them to have someone they can confide in, someone who they feel is on their side and has their best interests at heart.

If people do not trust their priests, they may not feel comfortable opening up about their fears and concerns, which can prevent the priest from being able to provide the support and guidance they need. However, when trust is established, people are more likely to be honest and open about their struggles and challenges, and the priest can provide guidance that is tailored to their unique situation.

> "*The presence of a faithful partner can be a great source of support and strength during a time of transition*"

Furthermore, trust allows for a deeper level of engagement between the person and the priest. It creates an environment where people feel comfortable sharing their deepest thoughts and feelings, and where the priest can offer guidance and support that is both practical and spiritual. This can help people to feel less alone in their journey and more confident in their ability to navigate the challenges of the transition process.

Don't be distracted by the irony of having to use 'competent' to qualify a Priest. You need to understand that transitions aren't the time for blind loyalty or trial and error. It takes one who has gone through similar transitions or one who is humble and generous enough to hold your hand, help piece together your broken heart and bring clarity to your confusion, for you to understand what you are going through.

In addition to being trustworthy, the competence of the priest is crucial when seeking guidance during a time of transition because it ensures that people receive sound knowledge and experience. A competent priest has the knowledge and training necessary to help people navigate the challenges of a major life change, such as a career shift, a move to a new city, or a significant loss.

A competent priest has the expertise necessary to provide practical and spiritual guidance that is tailored to the unique needs and challenges of the individual. This can include things like offering resources for job searching, providing counseling for grief or loss, or helping people to find spiritual practices that support their personal growth and development.

Moreover, a competent priest is well-versed in the scriptures and teachings of the faith, which enables them to offer guidance that is grounded in a deep understanding of the faith. This can be particularly important for people who are seeking to connect with their faith during a time of transition or uncertainty.

At a point in my life, I had to open up to my Pastor, trying to convince him to change his mind and give someone else the responsibility he had given me because I thought I was going to disappoint him. After my emotional outburst, he said the following words that changed my life; "PI, this church belongs to God, not to me. If you 'disgrace' God, then let Him deal with you and clean up the mess. After all, He is God, and it is His church." As simple as these words are, I wouldn't be wrong to say that they formed the basis for me to carry out God's plan for my life.

No matter how sincere a priest (one who has authority over you) is, mere sincerity can only identify with you in your pain, with little or no contribution to your progress. You shouldn't despise them either, rather focus on finding one who can provide wisdom and direction to help you navigate the seasons of your life. You might be perturbed by stories of other people's experiences in such situations, but you shouldn't be discouraged. Seek help prayerfully and be discerning.

## 2. FAITHFUL PARTNERS

The presence of a faithful partner can be a great source of support and strength during a time of transition. Faithful partners can offer a listening ear, practical support, and emotional encouragement when navigating the challenges of a major life change.

> *"Open and honest communication is also crucial to restoring a relationship after a transition"*

One of the most important ways that a faithful partner can help during a transition is by providing a listening ear. Transitions can be overwhelming and confusing, and it can be helpful to have someone who is willing to listen and offer support. A faithful partner can provide a safe space for people to express their fears, doubts, and hopes without fear of judgment or criticism.

Additionally, a faithful partner can provide practical support during a time of transition. This can include things like helping with household tasks, providing financial support, or assisting with job searches. When facing major life changes, it can be difficult to manage all the practical details on one's own, and having a partner who is willing to lend a hand can be invaluable.

> *"One way to attract people who are willing to take a chance on you is to demonstrate your potential"*

Also, a faithful partner can provide emotional encouragement and support during a time of transition. The process of change can be emotional and challenging, and it can be helpful to have someone who can offer words of encouragement and support when things get tough. A faithful partner can help people to stay focused on their goals and to keep moving forward even when things seem difficult.

This isn't the time to make an issue out of who left the tap running or who forgot to pick up the kids from school, neither is it the time to keep records of who called/texted first or who didn't apologize. The transition itself is exhausting, and the last thing you need are partners who deplete you of life.

You need people who are mature enough to let you breathe, even as you're trying to handle the burden of your responsibility. This does not relieve you of your responsibilities, but you need people who see all things through the lens of love. A transition isn't when you can be assured that you'll always figure things out, so, you need people who would understand and respect your process enough to not be offended by the shortcomings your transition will create.

Having a faithful partner during a transition can be incredibly powerful. One of the key advantages of having a partner who is committed to working with you through the transition is the power of collaboration. When two people work together toward a common goal, the results can be far greater than anything either person could have achieved alone.

> *"Do not give room for naysayers to interpret seasons in your life"*

For example, if you and your partner are both working toward a successful transition, you can leverage each other's strengths and skills to accomplish more than you could on your own. You can support each other in times of doubt or uncertainty, and provide a sounding board for new ideas or strategies.

Collaboration also means that you can share the workload, allowing you to tackle challenges more efficiently and effectively.

This can be particularly important during times of transition, when there may be a lot of moving parts and new demands on your time and energy. Working together can help you stay organized, focused, and on track toward your goals.

In addition to this, the power of collaboration can help to build trust and strengthen your relationship. By working together and achieving shared goals, you and your partner can develop a sense of mutual respect and appreciation. You can learn to rely on each other, and build a foundation of trust that will serve you well in the future.

You need all the support and encouragement to focus on stewarding your seasons effectively, rather than quelling the fires of bruised egos and people's expectations of you.

If your partner is not supportive during a transition, it can be a difficult and challenging experience. However, here are four (4) steps you can take to cope and move forward.

1. **Communicate with your partner:** It is important to have an open and honest conversation with your partner about how their lack of support is affecting you. Share your feelings and concerns, and try to listen to their perspective as well. It is possible that your partner may not understand the impact their actions are having on you.

2. **Seek support elsewhere:** If your partner is not able or willing to support you during this time, it is important to seek support elsewhere. This can be through friends, family, or a professional counselor. Having a support system outside of your partner can help you navigate the transition and cope with any challenges that arise.

3. **Focus on self-care:** During a transition, it is important to prioritize self-care. This can include taking time for yourself,

engaging in activities that bring you joy, and focusing on your physical and emotional well-being. By taking care of yourself, you can build resilience and find the strength to move forward even if your partner is not supportive.

**4. Consider couples counseling:** If your partner is open to it, couples counseling can be a helpful way to work through issues in your relationship and build a stronger, more supportive partnership. A trained therapist can help facilitate communication and provide tools for addressing challenges. Restoring a relationship after a transition can be a challenging and sometimes painful process, especially when your partner couldn't understand or contribute to your journey, but it can also be an opportunity to strengthen your bond and move forward together in a positive direction.

> *"Boundaries help you maintain a sense of control over your life"*

To begin with, it is essential to take responsibility for any mistakes or missteps you may have made that contributed to the breakdown of the relationship. This may involve apologizing for any hurt you caused, acknowledging where you fell short, and being willing to work on yourself to prevent the same issues from recurring in the future. it is also important to avoid blaming your partner or getting defensive, as this can create further tension and damage trust.

Open and honest communication is also crucial to restoring a relationship after a transition. This may involve having difficult conversations about what went wrong and how you can move forward together. It may also involve listening actively to your partner's perspective and being willing to compromise and find a common ground.

It is important to be patient and compassionate with one another as you work through these issues, and to approach the process with a sense of humility and a willingness to learn and grow.

> *"Refuse to shortchange yourself over other people's smallness"*

For example, imagine that during a recent transition, you and your partner experienced a significant conflict, and your relationship suffered as a result. Now that the transition is over, you realize that you miss your partner and want to work on rebuilding your relationship.

You start by acknowledging the ways in which you contributed to the breakdown of the relationship, apologizing for any hurt you caused, and expressing your willingness to work on yourself and the relationship.

You then have a series of open and honest conversations with your partner about what went wrong, how you can move forward, and what each of you needs from the relationship. With time, patience, and effort, you and your partner are able to restore your relationship and move forward together in a positive direction.

### 3. TEACHERS OF THE WORD

The presence of a trusted priest doesn't rule out the need for an accurate diet of the word. While the strength of a trusted priest lies in their experience with similar transitions, the value of other ministry gifts, especially those who teach the word of God, lies in their ability to reveal God's will and His way from scriptures, to help you manage the seasons of your life.

> *"Our ability to think beyond ourselves is what draws divine attention to us"*

As like I said before, do not despise people because you feel they don't understand what you are going through. Truly, they may not, but it takes humility of heart to receive the proceeding word of God concerning your situation. God has given the body of Christ gifts for the edification of the saints, and you shouldn't starve in the presence of plenty. The fastest way to be replenished is to feast on the word from those who can rightly divide truth into pieces that nourish you with the life of God.

There is a tendency to stick to what you are familiar with. We all have our favorite preachers and those whose words resonate with us, but you need more than that. A sick person doesn't need just comfort, but the right cure for their ailment.

Transitions are so important that you need the word of God for the season to go through them accurately. Your commitment should be to God's Word for the season and not the preacher of the Season. Keep your preferences aside and search for truth.

It is the truth that makes you free, not what your ears are itching for. Do not give your insecurities the upper hand.

> *"Take the knowledge and experiences you have gained and apply them to new situations"*

**4. A COUNSELOR / THERAPIST**

One lady came to me to talk about what she was going through. During our conversation, I suggested that she meets with a professional Counselor or a Therapist. Following the typical African response, she hurriedly avoided me, asking if I was trying to imply that she had a psychological problem. Although the experience was not encouraging, I was not surprised.

We have come to believe that if it doesn't come from the four walls of the church, it isn't of God, but there is a level of understanding I want you to get to, by reading this book. They include;

- All knowledge and power belong to God.
- To help all creation access Him, regardless of their leanings, there is no monopoly on the wisdom of God.
- Although the Church is the custodian of the whole counsel of God, He distributed His wisdom across diverse areas of life, including nature.
- Science is a dimension of the wisdom of God.

God isn't intimidated by the dynamics of science; only the egos of men are.

> *"Your transition is the process of birthing God's will through your experiences"*

The sooner you accept this truth, the sooner you maximize the blessings of God. As you go through transitions, if you have access to professional advice, accept it with your full chest. God distributed His wisdom to foster interdependence. Don't let your unhealthy ego deny you help.

**5. PEOPLE WHO ARE WILLING TO TAKE A CHANCE ON YOU**

One crucial element in making successful transitions is having people who are willing to take a chance on you. These people are individuals who believe in your potential and are willing to support you even when you are not fully formed.

They are people who are willing to invest in you and give you opportunities that will help you grow and develop.

Having people who are willing to take a chance on you can be a game- changer when you are going through a transition. For instance, let's say you are trying to change careers, and you don't have the necessary experience or qualifications.

In such a situation, it is easy to get discouraged and feel like you will never get a chance to prove yourself. However, having someone who believes in you and is willing to give you an opportunity can make all the difference. They can help you get your foot in the door and provide you with the support you need to succeed.

> "Your obedience can also create a positive and supportive environment for your children"

Since you need to steward your transitions well, it matters how you come out of them. After leaving my assignment as Resident Pastor, adding to the fatigue of this season, I found myself trying to hang on to anything and everything. In 2016, during that season, I got a job with a non-profit organization in Lagos. If I have to count my blessings, that job would be the 99 before my 100. The organization was what I needed at that point, having had to battle the numbness that came with walking away from my former assignment. It allowed me to explore some things God was putting in my heart at the time, and the result was the birth of the ministry I now lead, the People of Influence Network.

It is okay to believe that I got the job because of my qualifications, but remember that I couldn't have been the most qualified, and I'm not even talking about an 'unmerited favor'. All I can say is that they were willing to allow me to rebuild. They weren't obligated to, but they gave me a platform to grow.

From experience, I believe that is one thing you must earnestly pray for. The fact is that people who are willing to take a chance on you are hard to come by. Many people are risk-averse and would rather go with the safe option. However, when you do find such individuals, it is important to cultivate and maintain those relationships. These people can be mentors, sponsors, or simply friends who believe in you. Your obedience can also create a positive and supportive environment for your children.

One way to attract people who are willing to take a chance on you is to demonstrate your potential. You can do this by being proactive in seeking out opportunities, taking on new challenges, and demonstrating a willingness to learn and grow.

When people see that you are serious about your goals and are willing to work hard to achieve them, they are more likely to take a chance on you. You wouldn't want to walk out of transitions into struggle. You need the favor of God through men and the humility to discern opportunities, to facilitate restoration in your new season.

**THE REALITY**

Believe me, if everyone had access to the five types of people I described earlier during their transitions, there would be no need to write this book. Relationships are shortcuts to accessing realms beyond your experience, however, oftentimes, what we need isn't what is available. Your ability to discern what is available, guard yourself where necessary and leverage opportunities for effective stewardship is what determines the fate of your transition.

## HOW TO MANAGE RELATIONSHIPS IN TRANSITIONS

### 1. THE EXPLOITATIVE NAYSAYERS

The presence of exploitative naysayers can greatly affect the fate of people's transitions. These are individuals who do not believe in your potential and may actively work to sabotage your efforts. They may discourage you from pursuing your dreams, belittle your accomplishments, and constantly point out your flaws.

Their negative attitude and behavior can create a toxic environment that saps your motivation and confidence. It can also lead to self-doubt and anxiety, which can prevent you from taking the necessary steps to move forward in your transition. In extreme cases, it can even lead to depression and other mental health issues.

The danger of exploitative naysayers lies in their ability to manipulate and control you, often in subtle ways. They may disguise their negative behavior as *"helpful advice"* or *"constructive criticism,"* but in reality, they are attempting to keep you down and maintain the status quo.

In the context of a transition, the presence of exploitative naysayers can be especially detrimental. It can cause you to doubt yourself and your ability to succeed in the new phase of life. It can also lead to missed opportunities, as you may be hesitant to take risks or pursue new opportunities due to fear of failure or criticism.

It is important to recognize the presence of exploitative naysayers and take steps to protect yourself from their negative influence.

Exploitative naysayers can gain access to you through various means such as social media, personal relationships, workplace interactions, or through their own network of acquaintances. They may use manipulative tactics such as guilt-tripping, gas lighting, or fear-mongering to sow doubt and confusion in your mind. They may try to undermine your confidence by highlighting your weaknesses or past mistakes, or by exaggerating the risks of the transition.

In some cases, they may even try to actively sabotage your efforts by spreading rumors or misinformation about you. it is important to be aware of the tactics these people use and to take steps to protect yourself from their influence.

In seasons of transition, you must learn how to define and give voice to your experiences, including your past. Do not give room for naysayers to interpret seasons in your life. Left alone, people will formulate strange theories and conspiracies to choke the seed of your past and rob you of the blessing it carries. After all, what good is a thing if it is polluted?

These people will make you believe that you are enemies with your past, and will go all out to demonize the systems, places, and people you left, while masquerading as an angel of light.

Be careful. Their goal is simple; attack your past to the point that you consider them an ally, because you are unable to control your emotions. The alliance they seek is an attempt to harness your kindness for personal gain, not that they are truly invested in your journey through life. To combat this, you must arm yourself with discernment and courage to decline "detrimental" support and stand alone, if need be. It is better to suffer alone than to be enslaved without purpose.

Protecting oneself from exploitative naysayers is crucial in ensuring a successful transition. The following are ways to safeguard oneself:

- **Be discerning:** it is essential to cultivate discernment when it comes to the people you allow into your life. Not everyone who comes your way, has your best interests at heart, and some may be actively seeking to harm or exploit you. Learning to discern who is trustworthy and who is not can help you avoid falling prey to exploitative naysayers. Take time to get to know people before trusting them and pay attention to any red flag that arises.
- **Set healthy boundaries:** Setting healthy boundaries is crucial to protecting yourself from people who would seek to take advantage of you. Boundaries help you maintain a sense of control over your own life, protect you from being taken advantage of, and ensure that you are only engaging with people who are respectful and supportive. Make sure to communicate your boundaries clearly and consistently and be willing to enforce them when necessary.
- **Learn to say no:** Saying "no" can be challenging, but it is an essential skill when it comes to protecting yourself from

people who would take advantage of you. You don't have to say yes to every request that comes your way, and learning to say no when something doesn't feel right is an important step in keeping yourself safe.

- **Surround yourself with supportive people:** Surrounding yourself with people who are supportive and uplifting can help protect you from exploitative naysayers. When you have a strong support network, you have people to turn to for guidance, advice, and comfort when things get tough. These people can also serve as a buffer against anyone who would seek to harm or exploit you.

## 2. THOSE WHO WON'T ACCEPT YOUR TRANSFORMATION

People who won't accept your transformation could include individuals who knew you before the transition, such as old friends, family members, or former colleagues. These individuals may struggle to see you in a new light, accept your new identity or behavior, and may try to undermine your progress by reminding you of your past mistakes or shortcomings. They may also resist your efforts to distance yourself from negative influences or environments.

Moreover, individuals who share different beliefs, values, or lifestyles may also struggle to accept your transformation. These individuals may see your changes as a threat to their own beliefs or way of life, or they may simply be uncomfortable with the changes that they see in you.

It is important to note that not all individuals who resist your transformation do so out of malice or ill intent. Some may genuinely be concerned for your well-being and may not understand the reasons behind your changes. However, regardless of the motivation behind their resistance, it can still be a hindrance to your progress.

They may try to persuade you to revert to your old ways or to return to previous environments or behaviors that were hindering your progress. They may also try to make you feel guilty or ashamed for making positive changes, or they may attempt to manipulate or control you through emotional appeals or other tactics.

These people know your story well. They may have been with you in the past season, or they may have done something with you. These people will be hesitant to adjust to your new experiences as God stirs up new circumstances around you, to prepare and position you for the next move. They will keep bringing up topics from your past to keep you busy, not minding how much you say you have moved on to new things. This is what we all have to go through after deciding to follow Jesus as our only goal. Regardless of the passion in our hearts and the effort we make, some people would still turn a blind eye to everything and insist on relating with us based on who we used to be. Even as close as our family, when we're trying to transition, they tend to disregard our process and label us for what they have always known us for.

Their negativity can affect your confidence and self-esteem. As you work to make changes in your life, it is important to have people who believe in you and encourage you. When those around you refuse to accept your transformation, it can lead to feelings of doubt and insecurity. You may start to question whether you are making the right choices, which can slow down your progress.

Again, they may try to pull you back into your old ways. If these individuals are used to the old version of you, they may try to keep you in that space because it is what they are familiar with. They may actively discourage you from making changes or try to sabotage your progress. This can be a real threat to your transition, as their efforts can be very persuasive, especially if you are feeling uncertain about your choices.

In retrospect to that, they may not be able to provide the support you need. As you go through a transition, you may need support in various ways, such as emotional support, advice, or accountability. If those around you don't support your transformation, they may not be able to provide the support you need. This can leave you feeling alone and unsupported, which can be detrimental to your progress.

Finally, their lack of acceptance can cause conflict and tension in your relationships. If you are going through a significant transformation, it is likely that your relationships will change as well. Some people may not be able to accept the new version of you, which can cause tension and conflict. If not handled well, this tension can damage your relationships, making it harder to navigate your transition successfully.

Your transition may be neutral, such as changing jobs, starting your own business, deciding to have a family, or relocating. Whatever it is, you will always meet someone who finds fault with your choices or refuses to come to terms with the reality of your new season. All you owe the people in your life is the burden of responsibility to communicate your transitions in a way they can understand, and be at peace with whatever they choose to do about it.

You don't have to convince people to accept your new season. Any attempt to do that could sabotage the process, seeing that you are one step away from pleasing people at the mercy of the move of God in your life. Respect and honor them enough to understand that although they served you in the previous seasons of your life, they aren't obligated to journey with you through your new season.

This is not to suggest that you 'cut people off', but if they choose to be occupied with the past, you should as well keep your eyes focused on maximizing seasons. Refuse to short-change yourself over other people's myopic perspective.

It is essential to set clear boundaries with such individuals clearly. You may need to limit or cut off contact with those who are actively trying to undermine your progress, or at the very least, reduce the amount of time you spend with them. it is important to surround yourself with individuals who support your transformation and encourage your growth, rather than those who hold you back.

To protect yourself from people who won't accept your transformation and may threaten the success of your transition, you can take the following steps:

- **Be confident in your transformation:** First and foremost, you need to have confidence in yourself and your transformation. When you are sure about the changes you have made and where you are heading, it will be easier to deal with those who won't accept your transformation.
- **Set clear boundaries:** it is essential to set clear boundaries with people who won't accept your transformation. Let them know what you will and will not tolerate, and stick to your boundaries. Be assertive, but also respectful and kind.
- **Surround yourself with supportive people:** Surround yourself with people who are supportive of your transformation and believe in you. These are the people who will encourage you, uplift you, and help you stay focused on your goals. Seek out like-minded individuals, join support groups, and connect with positive influences.
- **Communicate effectively:** Communication is key when dealing with people who won't accept your transformation. Be clear and concise about your thoughts and feelings, and actively listen to their perspective. Try to understand where they are coming from and share your point of view in a respectful and non-judgmental way. Avoid getting defensive or confrontational.

Remember, not everyone will understand or accept your transformation, and that's okay. What's important is that you stay true to yourself, focus on your goals, and surround yourself with people who support and uplift you.

## 3. FALSE TEACHERS

*Matthew 7:15, 20:*

*"Beware of false prophets, who come to you in sheep's clothing, but inwardly they are ravenous wolves. Therefore, by their fruits, you will know them."*

As we agreed in the previous section, transitions are when you need a well-cultured diet of the word, but the sensitivity of shifts requires heightened vigilance. You will likely come across those who use the Word to either swindle or distract you from what God is trying to make out of you.

The presence of false teachers can greatly affect the fate of people's transitions. False teachers are those who claim to have spiritual knowledge and insight but are actually deceivers. They may use manipulative tactics and false promises to gain followers and can lead people down the wrong path. False teachers can threaten the outcome of people's transitions by leading them astray from the truth and wisdom that is necessary to navigate the challenges of a transition successfully.

They may present distorted or incomplete teachings that don't align with the scriptures or promote self-serving interests that detract from God's plan for an individual's life. False teachers may also prey on the vulnerability and uncertainty that people may feel during a transition by presenting themselves as having all the answers or solutions.

As a result, people may be misled or distracted from the crucial steps that they need to take to achieve their goals and fulfill their purpose. False teachings can lead to confusion, doubt, and even more significant setbacks, making it harder for individuals to make the right decisions and pursue the opportunities that come with a transition.

False teachers may have charismatic personalities and appear to be sincere, but their teachings can be harmful and ultimately lead to destruction. They may distort the truth, promote a false gospel, or lead people into legalism or spiritual bondage. False teachers may also promote a message of self-centeredness or materialism, which can distract you from the true purpose and meaning of your life.

They may use persuasive language or emotional appeals to draw people in, but ultimately their teachings will lead to a dead end.

This is not the time to seek comfort in vain babbling and doctrines of men. As expected, there will be those who would use the Word to promote their agenda instead of the agenda of God. False teachers can be difficult to identify, but here are five (5) signs to watch out for:

- **Evaluate their teachings:** One way to identify false teachers is by carefully evaluating their teachings. False teachers often distort or misinterpret scripture to support their own agendas, rather than accurately conveying the true message of the Bible. it is important to be knowledgeable about the scripture yourself so that you can recognize when someone is taking it out of context or adding their own interpretations.

- **Look at their fruits:** Another way to identify a false teacher is by examining the fruit of their teachings. In other words, what kind of impact do their teachings have on the lives of those who follow them? Do their teachings lead to positive change and spiritual growth, or do they promote division, selfishness, and sin? If someone is claiming to be a teacher of God's truth, but their teachings are not producing good fruit, it is a warning sign.
- **Observe their character:** The character of a teacher is also important to consider. False teachers may appear to be very religious or pious on the outside, but their true character will eventually be revealed. Are they living a lifestyle that reflects the values they claim to be teaching? Are they honest and humble, or do they seem to be driven by pride and greed? A true teacher of God's truth will demonstrate Christ-like character in their words and actions.
- **Lack of accountability:** False teachers often lack accountability and may surround themselves with "yes-men" who won't question their teachings or behavior. They may also avoid any criticism or correction from others. This is a major red flag when identifying false teachers. False teachers are often not accountable to any higher authority or community, which means that they can teach whatever they want without any checks and balances.

They may not be accountable to a religious community, a governing body, or even to their own followers. This lack of accountability can lead to dangerous teachings and practices that can harm individuals and communities.

Without accountability, false teachers may not be held responsible for the consequences of their teachings and actions. They may be free to manipulate and exploit their followers for personal gain or to promote their own agenda. They may be unwilling to engage in honest dialogues or to consider differing opinions. This can create an echo chamber where their teachings go unchallenged and their followers become more and more entrenched in their beliefs, even if those beliefs are false or harmful.

- **Seek wise counsel:** Finally, seeking the advice and guidance of other mature and wise Christians can be a helpful way to identify false teachers. These may be pastors, elders, or other trusted leaders in your church or community.

By sharing your concerns with them and asking for their input, you can gain valuable insights and perspectives that can help you identify any false teachings or teachers that you may encounter. It is important to remember that no one is infallible, so seeking the advice and guidance of others can help you avoid being deceived by false teachers.

In transitions, you must learn to submit to God, even in your pain and confusion, and you don't need words that make you complacent or cause you to dishonor seasons in your life. To protect yourself from false teachers who can threaten the success of your transition, here are five (5) steps you can take:

- **Be knowledgeable:** Educate yourself on what the Bible teaches about specific doctrines and issues. This way, you will be better equipped to identify false teachings when you encounter them.
- **Be discerning:** Do not just accept everything you hear from any teacher or preacher. Evaluate everything based

on what the Bible says. If something doesn't align with the scripture, it may be a false teaching.

- **Seek accountability:** Surround yourself with a community of believers who can hold you accountable and provide you with support and guidance in your spiritual growth.
- **Test the spirits:** As 1 John 4:1 says, *"Do not believe every spirit, but test the spirits to see whether they are from God."* This means examining the character and teachings of those who claim to be speaking on behalf of God. Look for consistency in their message and their life.
- **Pray for discernment:** Ask God to give you the discernment you need to identify false teachings and to guide you in your spiritual growth. The Holy Spirit can help you discern truth from lies.

By taking these steps, you can protect yourself from false teachers and ensure that your transition is rooted in truth and guided by the Holy Spirit.

The best way to stay away from false teachers is by cultivating a private life of fellowship so much that you understand God's opinion on what is going on, and only pay attention to the vessels through whom He chooses to elaborate and bring perspective to how you can accurately steward seasons.

## 4. THOSE WHO NEED YOUR BATTLE SCARS

It is easy to get carried away by your need for support and encouragement during your season of transition, that you neglect your call to service. Come to think of it, the greatest pillar of our salvation was erected during the greatest suffering of our Savior. His attention wasn't only fixed on the

Father to save Him from the pain, but His heart was set on the restoration and transformation of man. Even in times of despair, our ability to think beyond ourselves is what draws divine attention to us.

After all of Israel was rejoicing for David's victory over Goliath, you would think that it was his red-carpet reception to royalty, seeing that he had been anointed already. The following years of David's life were spent in caves and valleys, fleeing the wrath of Saul.

At a point, God delivered him from a spear that Saul had maliciously released to pin David to the wall. How much help can one who is cautious of his every move, surviving one plot after the other, give? Shouldn't he be scouting for spies and allies, to wage a counterattack against Saul?

*1 Samuel 22:1-2:*

*"David left Gath and escaped to the cave of Adullam. When his brothers and his father's household heard about it, they went down to him there. All those who were in distress or debt or discontented gathered around him, and he became their commander. About four hundred men were with him."*

Those we would ordinarily consider liabilities in a war, with diverse challenges, came to submit to David, and he became their commander. Regardless of his problems, he didn't just welcome them and leave them to fend for themselves. He accepted responsibility for their welfare and development. Nobody said he was obligated to do that or that God commanded him to, but he understood that his ability to steward whatever life brings to him, choosing to not sulk in his pain, would define the outcome of his transition.

Over time, out of those who we could have written off as destitutes, he raised those we call David's Mighty Warriors. He didn't have any particular assurance that convinced him that his investment in them was viable, neither did he bind them to any oath as proof of their unwavering loyalty, yet he took a chance with them and those men turned out to be all the support and strength he needed on his journey to the Throne and during his reign as king.

When I received the instruction to start the *People of Influence Network*, I imagined that God was sending me to top-level executives, captains of industries, legislators, and all those in positions of authority and influence. After we began the vision, God kept bringing people in their lowly state, young and in need of direction. They did not look anything like our expectations.

As we remain committed to doing His will, we realize that He is indeed raising a people of influence from among us, and we are humbled by it all. In your seasons of despair, you will meet with those who, although you might be tempted to classify their situation as nothing different from yours, you know that even in your pain and confusion, you can be their source of strength and direction. Even in your weariness, be not weary in well doing.

**ADMISSIONS**

As you try to make sense of what you are going through, you would have to admit that there were things you didn't do well and others that you could have done differently.

Notwithstanding the need to understand what happened or what God is doing through it, you also need to understand your role in everything. You need to evaluate your actions and inactions that could have brought you here.

Here are three areas you need to be true to yourself:

## 1. YOU ARE NOT BLAMELESS

In transitions, we are most likely to be plunged into so much confusion that we act as though it all happened suddenly, without our notice. The truth is that, at some point, we could have made the transition earlier. The dynamics of transitions are the result of God's intervention when we become too complacent to yield to His instructions.

*Amos 3:7:*

*"Surely the Sovereign Lord does nothing without revealing his plan to his servants the prophets"*

From this, we understand that there is no lack of the wisdom of God; only people who either won't seek or won't yield at the instance of the instruction. Even when we hear the voice of God audibly, most of the time we are paralyzed with fear. It is possible that fear robbed you of your ability to control your experiences, and prevented you from assessing things accurately, leaving you focused on trying to manage what you were used to, until God orchestrated the shaking.

When it is not fear that is holding you back, then it is your affection and attachment to the previous season of your life that is holding you back. It is one thing to think of lust as a mere want or desire, but this definition might end up making those who are guilty of the spirit of lust complacent.

Lust is an exaltation of convenience, out of the confidence you have in yourself and your ideas, over the character of God to do new things in line with His agenda for your life. You have to admit the fears and lusts that kept you from moving as you receive instructions. Could it be that you trusted in your former season more than the God who brought you into it? Were you too cautious not to lose what God helped you achieve? These are things you would have to admit to yourself.

## 2. YOU COULD HAVE STEWARDED THE PROCESS BETTER

Recognizing and acknowledging your emotions during a transition is important, but it is also essential to understand that your pain is not a justification for hurting others. Just because you may be facing challenges or difficulties during this change, it doesn't give you the right to lash out or treat others poorly. it is important to remain respectful and considerate, even when you're feeling overwhelmed or frustrated.

It is also important to remember that the systems, places, and people you are leaving behind may not be inherently bad. They may have served a purpose in your life and played a role in your growth and development. However, they may also have had faults that were preventing you from reaching your full potential and fulfilling God's plan for your life. This is why transitions are necessary, as they allow you to move forward and continue growing.

By acknowledging your emotions and the role that systems, places, and people have played in your life, you can approach transitions with a more positive and constructive attitude. You can focus on what you have learned from these experiences and how you can use this knowledge to create a better future for yourself. In this way, transitions can become an opportunity for growth, rather than a source of stress or frustration.

You would have to acknowledge how much they contributed to your progress. You have to be intentional about it, to cut through your emotions. Be humble enough to also admit that you were not perfect. If you were, there won't be a need to take you through a transition. Transitions are God's attempt to bring us to perfection, if we would yield ourselves.

Admitting that there were better ways to manage previous seasons of your life is a crucial step in personal growth and self-reflection. it is easy to look back on the past and think that everything was perfect, but the reality is that there are always ways to improve and make better decisions.

Recognizing this and admitting that you didn't know better can be difficult, as it requires humility and self- awareness. However, it is a critical step in your journey toward growth and personal development. By acknowledging that there were better ways to manage your life, you can learn from your mistakes and make better choices in the future.

This doesn't mean that you should beat yourself up or dwell on the past, but rather, use these lessons to create a better future for yourself. You can take the knowledge and experiences you have gained and apply them to new situations, making more informed and thoughtful decisions. In this way, admitting that you didn't know better can be a powerful tool for personal growth and self- improvement. It allows you to take responsibility for your actions and use the lessons from the past to create a brighter and more fulfilling future.

## 3. YOU HAVE WORK TO DO

Do not be in a hurry to arrive at a destination. Your transition is the birthing of God's will through your experiences, and your willingness to work with God determines the success of the transition. As a result of your time and integration in the previous season, there is still cultural residue from that season residing in you even though you may be unconscious of it.

The Israelites, for instance, seemed like people who were devoted to following God through the transition, however, they were still attached to the culture of Egypt. On the surface, it appeared as though all they took from Egypt were material things such as gold, silver and other valuables, and, possibly, every negative reality Egypt had to offer was drowned in the Red Sea. But internally they had imbibed the ways of Egypt.

Without a doubt, you want to move on and forget about the past, but you would be surprised to find out that your appetite for cucumber and onions will deprive you of the glory of a land of milk and honey if you do not take intentional steps to unlearn the culture of the previous season. You may not have had any problems in the previous season, but the pain of moving may just be what is holding you back. Your commitment should be to do away with whatever the Lord doesn't desire in the new season, regardless of how it came.

*Chapter 8*

# MY BLUEPRINT FOR MAKING SUCCESSFUL TRANSITIONS

*In order to maximize this season, you need to admit that you are not the 'eternal well of wisdom'. You do not know all you need to know, hence you need other people. You need God to teach and train you. This will redefine how you see the change you need to go through.*

## *Chapter 8*

# MY BLUEPRINT FOR MAKING SUCCESSFUL TRANSITIONS

Sometimes, we may be aware that God is moving us and we are in a transition, however, feelings and emotions like pain, shame, and inadequacies (e.g. imposter syndrome), often attached to the process make it challenging for us to accept what the Lord is doing in/through/for us.

There are times we may even resist the change that the Lord is producing in our lives.

One of the ways we can partner with God in a time of transition is to keep our eyes on:

- What God is doing
- What we should be doing

At every transition, there are different classes of what to focus on. These include:

God, the Author, and Finisher of our faith: Given the fact that He is the one who brings veritable context into everyone's transition and He is the one that everyone is transiting into, there is no transition we are making in this life that is made outside of God or outside the strength of who God is.

You, the one who is making the transition: You have to be able to keep your eye on what God is doing and also keep your eye on what you should be doing. Do not get overwhelmed by the things that are in God's hands, but focus on the things that are in your hands because God will certainly not renege on His promises nor fail in His responsibilities. However, it is possible for you to fail in your responsibilities. One of the things you should be doing is permitting the process to change, transform and birth in you. Allow the process to sort things out and change who you are from within.

## ACKNOWLEDGE INADEQUACIES

Sometimes, the very reason we struggle to change is that we do not acknowledge the fact that we are not everything; we cannot be everything. We struggle with our inadequacies, not realizing that, sometimes, it is God who puts those inadequacies in us so that we can stretch our hands and ask for help, and have someone else help us through the journey of life.

> *"Sometimes, it is God who puts those inadequacies in us so that we can stretch our hands and ask for help"*

In order to maximize this season, you need to admit that you are not the 'eternal well of wisdom'. You do not know all that there is to know hence you need other people. You need God to teach and train you. This will redefine how you see the change you need to go through.

There is the lie of the enemy that makes us believe that God doesn't want to hear our struggles. We may feel like admitting to God may make it awkward and we end up not addressing situations. We must remember that there are no challenges, iniquity, or shortcomings we have that intimidate God, but instead, we are the ones intimidated. We must remember that God is our Father and He is always open, ready, and willing to help us through the situations of our lives.

Say it to yourself, but not only as a single statement. Make sense of it by expanding on why you are limited.

- Admit how you feel by articulating/writing it down.
- Making scriptural references further explain the situation e.g., the habit of stealing and what the bible says about stealing. By doing this you are addressing and attacking the weakness and seeing the root of it

> *"Prayer is not just an act. It is an exchange of substance"*

- Who does God say that you are? - Countering the lie of the enemy by the light of the Word.

This allows us to introspect and see areas where we may be missing. By doing this, God reveals things to us that may even trigger some of these character flaws and habits. During such a time, we should also stay in prayer and not be afraid to question everything; every emotion we feel, every discomfort, the questions raised in our hearts, every pondering or uncertainty, everything.

> *"What makes it possible for your prayer to change you is that you have a burden"*

It is in this curiosity that we begin the journey of going deeper into the matter. Do not be afraid to shake those tables. This also helps us not just to see the truth of who we are but also the truth of who the enemy is, it reveals to us and reminds us of his perdition.

Next is to identify the things that you are, the things you have, and the things that you do well. Think of it like a SWOT ANALYSIS. What areas are you at your best? What environments bring out the best in you? What conversations, places, or situations allow you to thrive?

Identify the things that you are not and identify the people/places/systems that are the things you are not. Simply because you are in a place of wanting change and having acknowledged that you do not have all the wisdom in the world, the acknowledgment in itself enables you to go through the process.

The moment you are able to identify the above, then you have to celebrate them spiritually, physically, and emotionally. When you celebrate it while praying, it is doing something to your mind and body; it is opening you up and placing in you what you need to evolve.

**PRAY**

Prayer is not just an act; it is an exchange of substance. Every time you pray, you are depositing something and also receiving something. When you pray, give your substance and wait for the release of His substance. Give your heart, your burdens, and troubles, and allow for the divine exchange that happens in the place of prayer. Always wait for the release of God's substance over you.

> *"Burdens are fuel for prayer"*

You must know that this is a process, and not just a moment. Many times, we talk about changing but forget that it is a process that doesn't happen overnight. Pray, knowing that God is working things out, even though the outcome may not be immediate.

We pray because we know we are being transformed, not just the hope of being transformed. The transformation of your spirit does not have a physical component; hence, the central objective of the transformation is to arrive at a point in the spirit where it is so great that it breaks through the barriers of your spirit and enters into your physical realm.

While the process is ongoing, do not be deceived by the enemy into thinking that nothing is happening in the realm of the spirit. Know that this change is happening, but it is a process. Pray with a burden to change. If you do not have a burden, pray till you receive it, then navigate through the burden using the light of truth as your compass.

What makes it possible for your prayer to change you is that you have a burden. When you go into the place of prayer and you do not have a burden, pray for a burden. Acknowledge that you are not in the right frame of mind to arrive at the place God desires for you to be. Such a posture of humility renders it possible for God to put His burden on you.

> *"Every time you fall on your knees, be ready to return with nothing that you went in with"*

When you receive the burden in prayer, do not let it overwhelm you. Yes, burdens can be overwhelming, because it is fuel for prayer. Your burden is also supposed to be a sort of light and navigation tool for you. As you pray, you are gauging the burden to determine if you are where you are supposed to be, per time.

As you pray, juxtapose it with scripture and check it with the Holy Ghost to know how you are doing. As you pray for change, allow yourself to be articulate because, many times, we are waiting for God to speak to us, but God usually speaks through us. You need to trust that, even in the place of prayer, you are a vessel, an oracle unto yourself. While you pray, God can use you to speak to you. You begin to declare and speak what is happening to you in the realm of the spirit.

Don't hide any part of you. Many people do not know how to be naked before God. We shouldn't play games with God. When you come before Him, take it all off and admit all; the brokenness, shame, iniquity, etc.

> *"The energy generated from the place of prayer should help you make decisions"*

There are times when being true translates into echoing the things that God is saying about you, it is to confess to yourself what God has confessed concerning you.

Sometimes, we do not confess what God has said about us because of our own self-righteousness. Open it all up and do not be afraid of what you will see or what God will show you because the whole idea is that we want to arrive at a state of Truth. We do not want Truth to be only a thing that is said to us by God, but a state that we operate in.

By this understanding, when I expose my heart to God and the deficiency of my spirit, what I am doing is taking the weapon from the hands of the enemy: my weakness is no longer an arsenal in the hand of Satan because I have taken the weakness and placed it in the hands of the Lord. It now becomes God's responsibility to transform me from that point forward, and that's why we expose it all to the Lord. The Lord then begins to show us the little steps we are to take, to enable us to arrive at wholeness.

> *"Never 'fake it till you make it' with things that have to do with destiny"*

Be prepared to lose everything in prayer because, sometimes, when you go in, nothing comes out on the other side but your refined spirit. Every time you fall on your knees, be ready to return with nothing that you went in with. The Lord will strip every load we come in with, in the place of prayer, one after the other. Be ready to lose it all.

Never go into prayer without the Holy Spirit. Hold the Holy Ghost and feel Him, because you are walking in a realm that you are not attuned with. As God takes you into different places, realms, dimensions, and areas you are not used to, you need the Holy Ghost to tell you where to go, when to pause, and what not to say, because He is the one that knows the intentions of God's heart. As you pray, make sure you have faith, because you need to be able to trust everything that you see, hear and experience in the place of prayer. Trust your sight and vision - everything that the Lord shows you while you pray. Trust it and have faith to believe those pictures because, sometimes, we arrive at the change, first, in the spirit before we arrive at it in the physical, and God will show us those changes in the form of pictures and visions, and you need to trust that.

Also, look out for blueprints and navigation tools because they are the very things that you will use as a guide for the life of who you are supposed to be, which God shows you in the place of prayer.

While you pray, carry your journal and pen, because, when you pray, you shift your spirit into the frequency of heaven, and when you do that, you are bound to hear things that you did not plan to hear, as God touches on every area and aspect of your life. These blueprints that you receive in prayer become the guide that helps you in your season of transition to know whether you are right or wrong and in what direction you are moving.

> *"Do not do things that aren't a product of the instructions you've achieved in the spirit"*

**MOVE**

Remember that prayer is an ever-continuous movement of a man's spirit toward the movement of God's spirit, and that is why you must **PRAY WITHOUT CEASING.** Every time we pray, we are continuously moving into the spirit of God and His perfection.

As we pray, we generate the energy for movement so we have to move. If you are going to change, then you must go beyond praying, and act on the things you receive in prayer. The purpose of prayer is not to have a pity party with the hosts of heaven, but for momentum to move. When you pray, the energy generated from the place of prayer should help you make decisions. The decisions you could not make before, prayer emboldens you to make them. These movements are marks of progress and are made on different levels. There are small, medium, and large scales of progress.

> *"Instead of seeing repetition as failure, consider it as an opportunity for mastery"*

Do not try to take all the medium leaps at once; just one change at a time.

For a start, it may be the grace and capacity to change the way you talk, meanwhile what you may want is to become a better entrepreneur. God may begin by changing the way you talk, then next, how you spend money and you begin to see every amount of money with value, then you begin to save, etc. These changes do not have to happen all at once.

Also, know that this movement will happen in all the realms; not just in the physical but in your spirit and soul. All realms are connected, and the reason why some people are not able to move at the time that they should move is that there is a disconnect between their body, soul, and spirit.

After generating so much power in the place of prayer, because of the brokenness of their spirit, they are unable to transfer this power to the physical. You must recognize the movements that should precede the declaration of change that should happen in every realm of your existence, and it must happen in your soul too.

Sometimes even your physical body changes in alignment with the change you have acquired in the spirit—something happens to you. Look out for the changes that will happen in your soul which can make you a better person, physically.

As you go through this process, understand that you do not induce change; you become it. As your soul is healed, all about you will change because the growth is inside, and the strength and peace are from within.

> *"Repetition produces mastery and mastery dispels deception"*

When you want to change, do not fake it. Never 'fake it till you make it' with things that have to do with destiny. Be real with God. If you do not have it, you do not have it. If you are not it, you are not it. However, you don't have to rest there; strive to BECOME! You must make little changes in the direction of the huge change that you want to see.

Go back and check your study time, your habits, and your prayer life. Ask yourself if the effort you are putting in is enough to arrive at the person you want to be. You need to have those types of true and honest conversations with yourself. Do not do things that aren't a product of the instructions you've achieved in the spirit.

Ways to check your instructions:

- Confirm from the Word of God
- Confer with mentors God has put in your lives and paths (beware of the novelty complex)

**PACE YOUR TRANSFORMATION**

Commit to the process: you do not call it commitment until you have tried and withstood the urge to fall into previous patterns. It is called commitment because there were options and reasons for you to draw back, but you didn't - you kept going. So stay committed to the process.

**REPEAT**

Just because God has addressed a certain area in your life doesn't mean He won't address it again in the future. He is constantly repeating through a growth process. God will revisit things we thought we have outgrown in a previous season.

The mistake some believers make when God is repeating a season is that they think God is saying they have failed, but that's not it. However, God is saying, you are taking an upgraded lesson in the same area that you have grown in, to help you grow even further. After all, the Bible says that He prunes the branches that bear fruit so that they may bear even more fruit.

The goal has always been to bring you into the fullness of God. Your ability to succeed in this new level is dependent on how you study the patterns of your restoration in the previous level.

Take these patterns and bring them into a new season, and use them to equip yourself to do better in the new season.

Instead of seeing repetition as failure, consider it as an opportunity for mastery. God's protocol of developing you and making you an expert doesn't mean you failed. You handle the word, but you cannot handle the word until the word has handled you. Allow Him to handle you in the various aspects of life, so that when you see a similar occurrence that God the Father, the Spirit, and the Word have dealt with expertly, you can discern it from a distance and handle it from a place of strength.

Repetition produces mastery and mastery dispels deception. When you become a master at it, you can easily tell when there is a deficiency, regardless of how it is presented. You can easily tell when the image is broken because you have become a master at it. You will no longer fall into the power of deception when you become a master of the process of life.

## *Chapter 9*

# THE WAY FORWARD

*The purpose of every seed is to produce root, shoot, leaves, and fruit, and you must understand that the fruit of bitterness is hatred. How do we show God's love when we fill our hearts with hatred?*

# Chapter 9

# THE WAY FORWARD

There will always be times in our journey of life when God would try to stretch us beyond what we are used to, into what He is calling us to become. Transitions are seasons that trigger the release of promises, but your ability to steward your transitions effectively is what guarantees that you come to the fullness of the promise.

The dynamics of transitions can be overwhelming because they come so suddenly. However, your ability to understand and give voice to your experiences is what gives you the advantage for lasting victory. Note that it is not enough to just understand or to give voice: what use is it to understand what is going on and still be helpless? Or is it better to try to make progress without making sense of what is before you?

> *Words of affirmation without understanding your truth will always leave you frustrated in the long run.*

Words of affirmation without understanding your truth will always leave you frustrated in the long run. Transitions often seem insurmountable, because, on your journey, you find yourself making multiple transitions while trying to make sense of the major transition. Your advantage lies in understanding what you are going through. It lies in your ability to see God in the midst of it, to see what He is trying to make out of you through your experiences, and your readiness to yield to His will and way.

Transitions are beyond the seasons we go through. They are meant to be encounters that empower us to serve the will of God effectively, without recourse to selfishness. The fragility of a transition lies in the fact that we may become so attached to the past that out of fear, ignorance, or desire, we may abandon God's next move.

During transitions, you are vulnerable to attacks and judgment, even from those you least expect. The reality of having to change without their permission will trigger their humanity to attack what God is doing with you, but you need to sustain the maturity to know that they don't hate you. They are just disturbed by the fact that you are no longer the person they know, and since they can no longer relate with you at that level, their frailty resorts to judgment. Not everyone knows what you are going through, even if it affects them. Instead of being petty and craving sympathy, it is your responsibility to communicate your transitions with those who have responsibility for you and those you are responsible for.

> *"Not everyone knows what you are going through, even if it affects them"*

In seasons of transition, close relationships are threatened, including marriages. That isn't the time to count scores or repay unfair treatment. Use the process to get closer. You need all the strength and support you can get at that point, and you don't want your partner to be what depletes your courage. You must master the art and act of communicating with people on different levels in a way that doesn't dishonor your transition or the people you relate with.

Provided you are committed to carrying people along, those who find it difficult to accept your new reality, after every attempt to make it clear to them, might as well become part of the things you should transit from.

> *"Don't get too used to how God moves that you forget that you must follow Him without getting attached to His acts"*

While God plans to work in and through you, you are responsible for what you make out of your transitions. Don't get carried away with the onions and garlic of Egypt or the pleasures and treasures of Sodom that you sacrifice the honor and glory of serving the next move of God.

Don't get too used to how God moves that you forget that you must follow Him without getting attached to His acts. Don't turn your brook and raven - your seasons of survival— into your rest. God's plan for the new season will be fulfilled, no matter what you do during the transition period, but what you do will determine your experience in the new season.

There is more to you than where you are from, and you need to be careful of anyone trying to keep you in the same position. They may seem harmless, but anything that doesn't move you toward God's next step, no matter how lucrative it may seem, will keep you away from God's will.

> *"It takes maturity to understand that you are not the only one who has been hurt"*

You must move at the speed of God's direction, but you must be careful of those who despise your yesterday. People that would want to exploit you by demonizing what you are coming out of are no angels themselves.

It takes maturity to understand that you are not the only one who has been hurt. Those who you left are hurting also.

Whichever way, you will have to forgive them. Do not let the seed of bitterness take root in your heart. The purpose of every seed is to produce root, shoot, leaves and fruit, and you must understand that the fruit of bitterness is hatred. How do we show God's love when we fill our hearts with hatred?

It would have been better if it was as easy as I have said, but there are three things you must do to get rid of bitterness:

**1. YOU MUST BE CLEAR ABOUT HOW YOU FEEL**

Do not be in a hurry to heal or deny how you feel. Try to process the pain and understand what exactly is going on. Do you feel betrayed? Does it feel like you were used and people took advantage of you? Do you feel denied of something you deserve?

Ask these questions until you get a clear picture of how you feel. You cannot defeat an enemy you don't understand.

## 2. BE CLEAR ABOUT THE ROLE YOU PLAYED IN GETTING HERE

It is easy to blame everyone but ourselves, but the truth is that we are not guiltless. At best, we are complicit in our fate.

> *"You cannot defeat an enemy you don't understand."*

Accept that you could have left or made the transition earlier. You might have been held back by fear and your attraction to the pleasures of your past.

Is there a better way to have handled everything? What if you knew better, would it have gotten to this level? Your lack of commitment to improving your discernment and hearing the voice of God could be what held you back.

The fact that you found yourself in that place and you stayed there long enough to be broken by the experience says a lot about you. Agree that you are not perfect. Deal with the fact that you are too comfortable in hiding and seclusion that God's attempt to get you out has left you disillusioned.

Carefully evaluate your actions and inactions accurately, to find out what you could have done differently. In transitions, your insecurities and the impact of your background are likely to be exposed, and you must be intentional about managing them.

## 3. HAVE A CLEAR VISION OF WHERE GOD IS TAKING YOU

Your ability to see things from an eternal perspective helps you handle pain better because your mind is fixated on things that are more real than what you are going through. You can see how all things work toward taking you to what God put in your heart. While this is beneficial, it is possible to get carried away with false humility and inverted pride, which could be part of what you identify as the role you played in it all.

At this stage, I believe you deserve to be applauded for coming this far on this journey. Irrespective of what you are dealing with and how many people are involved, it remains your responsibility to find strength and direction in everything, and make progress with your life.

Yes, it was an experience you were committed to at the time. Yes, it served you throughout its existence and you won't mind sticking with it much longer. As you found out in this book, you are not alone. it is a general experience that even I have to deal with. You might assume that "Oh, it is Apostle Isi. She's got everything figured out." But that is not exactly the case. As I write this, in October 2022, we just concluded a major apostolic and prophetic women's conference in South Africa. When we first started the ministry—*People of Influence Network*, it quickly became clear that the time would come when we would have to take our mission to other countries.

Don't get it twisted, I am not new to traveling. For what it is worth, God has helped us greatly, and we are fortunate enough to be able to travel when we need to. However, there is a vast difference between simply traveling for a holiday or something else and then traveling to host a women's conference on the scale of the Mantle of Deborah multiple times in a year.

For a regular trip, you wouldn't need more than your tickets, accommodation, and enough money to cover your expenses while you are away. While the two have the basic characteristics of international travel in common, our regular international holidays obviously cannot be compared with the volume of work that encompasses an international event that has over 1,000 registrations.

The planning for logistics, feeding, venue, media, and all it entails, including undertaking the requisite spiritual preparation to be a blessing to people comes with its own peculiar set of challenges. We had fasting and prayer programs all through October, toward the conference, and you can envisage the intensity of it all. Yes, the event was a success, but there were nights when it honestly felt as though we were not ready to hold the conference.

> *"Your ability to see things from an eternal perspective helps you handle pain better"*

As overwhelming as some of the days got, we prevailed largely because I put to use the strategies I have outlined in this book.

We had a number of hurdles to overcome in the planning process and several little fires we had to put out. The issues we faced were not as a result of not knowing what to do per se, mind you, we had hosted the same conferences in Nigeria and Kenya prior to the time. All we needed was the strength to pull through the South Africa edition.

All through our somewhat "turbulent take off", what kept us strong on our flight path was the knowledge of what God wanted to achieve through the conference and the conviction that we could not let our shortcomings short-change that.

It was powerful to realize that these principles I first learned in 2020 continue to produce solid results in 2022, and that inspired me to finally publish this book. Why should you be held back by experiences you don't understand when you should be making progress? Yes, life happens, but that should not mean the world has to come to a grinding halt. You must be ready to definitively apply the strategies you have received from this book to create the life you want for yourself.

> *"The validity of your pain doesn't automatically bequeath relief."*

Do not get so carried away with the excitement of reading a good book that you forget to actually make your life better. Make it a non-negotiable point to willfully and prayerfully incorporate these principles into your life.

Dare to leave "here" so you get "there" and you bet I will be on the other side of "there", rallying you to your next victory!

## THREE TOOLS FOR SUCCESSFUL TRANSITIONS

### 1. JOURNALING

Habakkuk 2:1 (NIV):

*"I will stand at my watch and station myself on the ramparts; I will look to see what he will say to me, and what answer I am to give to this complaint."*

During the transition, the position you take is important. The pain and confusion you feel will tend to overwhelm you and prevent you from finding a way out. The validity of being intentional about searching for God's way out of the challenge. In your disillusionment, you must rid your heart of bitterness, vengeful thoughts, and everything that occupies and keeps you away from your solution. You must pay attention to what God is saying about your challenge. God responds to only those whose hearts long for Him and His word, not necessarily those who need it. As you try to make sense of what is happening, let your heart be fixed.

> *"Clarity brings understanding and strength for pursuit"*

Habakkuk 2:2 (NIV):

*"And the LORD answered me, and said, Write the vision, and make it plain upon tables, that he may run that readeth it."*

As you pay attention to understanding what God is doing in this season, it is your responsibility to document your experiences. The power of the Word is not in its availability. It is possible to receive the Word of God on a matter and still be trapped in your experiences.

What assures you of success is how much of the Word you understand. One proven way to accurately understand God's mind on an issue is to write it down as simply as you understand it. If you can express what you feel, what God is saying, what God is trying to achieve, and what He expects you to do, you will receive the strength to run.

> *"Peace and clarity are the tools with which we go through transitions"*

Clarity brings understanding and strength for pursuit. The reality is that, even when others with similar experiences look at your life and how you managed this season, they will find strength in the things you documented, and run with it. It will be your testimony of God's faithfulness in the days to come.

As you go through the seasons of your life, you need to learn how to document the workings of God. Writing helps you process, identify and express your thoughts and feelings with clarity and power. It helps you put your feelings before you, for proper evaluation.

Write down what He is saying and what He is quiet about, what He is intercepting, and what He is permitting. In the days to come, this would be a strong source of clarity as to where God has brought you from and where He is taking you. Write down the prophecies you receive —both as God gives them directly to you or through other vessels. If you don't know what to write, just write down how you feel. At least, they will serve as testaments of God's commitment to you. Write down what you can make of what is happening. Write down what you did and what you could have done differently.

Write down the people and parties involved and define the new terms of engagement because malice and strife are not options. Be sure to make sense and give voice to everything you go through, starting with writing them down.

> *"Courage and peace are things we receive in the place of intimacy with the Holy Spirit"*

## 2. CONSTANTLY POUR OUT YOUR HEART TO GOD

Since we are bound to be overwhelmed and disillusioned by transitions, it is not the time to sulk. Peace and clarity are the tools with which we go through transitions. It is easy to want to 'sulk in peace', but you must ask yourself, how much peace you get from sulking? In John 14:27, Jesus made it clear that peace is the fruit of fellowship.

The enemy can usurp your transitions and sow seeds of fear and lack of peace. With fear, he takes away your ability to exert control over your experiences, distracts you from being able to evaluate things accurately, and leaves you focused on trying to live through your pain with little or no regard for how you can bless others.

On the contrary, we have received a spirit that imparts us with courage. The courage that goes beyond guts and gusto. Courage is the impartation of an understanding of the will of God about an issue, and the empowerment to pursue it. Both courage and peace are things we receive in the place of intimacy with the Holy Spirit. As you would know, God only confides in those who fear Him —Psalms 25:14.

In transitions, we must commit ourselves to constant communion with the Holy Spirit. Don't be too cautious to not pour out your heart to him, after all, we have a High Priest who isn't only touched by our shortcomings but has given us access to the Throne of Grace to receive help.

It is not enough for help to be made available; you will have to get yourself together and take your mess to the Throne by yourself. Sometimes, you might even have to discover His presence in a new way. Don't be limited by your commitment to a routine.

Spend every moment praying and in deep reverence for God and His ways. Soak yourself in the Word and worship. Don't forsake fellowship with the brethren; it is God's strategy for preservation.

Put a knife to your desires and dedicate your appetite to finding him. The most important thing is to have a heart posture that yearns for him enough, that time becomes inconsequential.

### 3. ALWAYS REMEMBER THE PURPOSE OF THE TRANSITION

While it is good to document your experiences as you grow and to maintain fellowship with the Holy Spirit, the goal is to accurately discern and keep in mind the purpose of the transition. If that is not achieved, you might get lost in cycles so much that you miss the move of God.

It takes more than identifying what you are going through to make sense of your experience. You need to understand what God is trying to birth in you. You must understand why it had to be now and this intense.

Where you fail to accurately discern the purpose of your transitions, you risk short-circuiting the agenda of God in the new season. You have to understand the limitations of your current experience and come to terms with the fact that what brought you here doesn't sustain the capacity to bring you into the fullness of God's will.

In this regard, you also have to be mature to understand that leaving a system, people, and places doesn't mean they are bad in themselves. The goal is to align with God's agenda. This would be your strength on the days when you can barely stand; your confidence in what God is doing with you will uphold you.

When you apply all the principles outlined in this book, you will see how you are able to go through your transition processes seamlessly.

## AFTERWORD

As individuals walking the path of faith, we are perpetual travelers, perpetually moving forward without looking back. The timeless adage, "forward ever, backward never," beautifully encapsulates this reality. At times, we find ourselves entrusted with a divine mandate to journey from our current position to an entirely new place or role. In such moments, our lives may feel disrupted, and we might grumble or even resist the call to move, for we have grown comfortable in our present circumstances. The idea of any disruption seems unwelcome, and we strive to maintain the status quo.

Navigating the transition phase proves arduous, yet within these pages, a compassionate guide awaits, poised to assist all who find themselves traversing similar paths. This book promises not only to offer guidance but also to ensure a seamless transition for those who not only read its contents but diligently follow the principles outlined within.

In my remarkable role as a spiritual leader, I transcend mere spiritual guidance and allow my profound understanding of the interconnectedness of every facet of life to permeate these pages, revealing that this book is not solely a compass for navigating the spiritual realm but also a trusted guide through the physical and psychological dimensions of our existence. This way, you are not only equipped with the spiritual tools that will help you in your transition process but also the physical, psychological and emotional tools that makes the process easier to go through.

# About the Author

Apostle Isi Igenegba is a visionary leader, minister of the Gospel, and a catalytic force for God's agenda in this season. With an unwavering commitment to advancing the Kingdom of God on earth, she carries a unique anointing and authority to ignite transformation, empower individuals, and effect positive change in diverse spheres of influence.

As the Lead of People of Influence Network and the visionary behind the Mantle of Deborah movement, Apostle Isi Igenegba has emerged as a prominent figure in the apostolic and prophetic landscape. Her divine assignment involves raising a generation of people who are catalysts for change, influencers in their respective fields, and manifesting the Life of God.

The Mantle of Deborah movement, birthed through divine inspiration, has gained tremendous momentum. Under her visionary leadership, the Mantle of Deborah movement has impacted people in nations across Africa, including Nigeria, Kenya, South Africa, Ghana and Botswana, and beyond. Through conferences, training programs, and retreats, thousands of women have been blessed, equipped, and empowered to pursue their God-given destinies. Lives have been transformed, businesses have been birthed and grown, and ministries have been ignited, all by the power of God.

With an unyielding faith in God's promises and a deep reverence for His Word, Apostle Isi Igenegba combines the power of her personal encounters with divine revelation to ignite radical transformation in the lives of individuals. Her ministry creates an atmosphere of divine impartation and supernatural encounters that propel individuals into their destinies.

With a profound understanding of the power of faith-based principles, business acumen, and social entrepreneurship,

Apostle Isi Igenegba has been instrumental in equipping and mentoring countless individuals across the globe. Her expertise lies in cultivating effective leadership, personal effectiveness, and relationship management, using a holistic approach that combines spiritual principles with practical strategies.

At Isi Benedicta Institute, she has dedicated herself to "retraining minds and rebuilding kings," imparting invaluable wisdom and tools to individuals from all walks of life. Apostle Isi equips people from all walks of life through training and courses tailored to bring solutions to various aspects of life, with her coaching and consulting expertise.

Some of her renowned publications include her books: From Here to There: Making Successful Transitions, Awaken to Your Purpose and Live, and her bestselling courses; The Shift and Awaken to Your Purpose. Isi Igenegba is the Founder of Sprouts Natural Foods and Lifestyle Products, a food manufacturing company with operations in Lagos and Canada, that seeks to promote healthy living through food, inspired lifestyle changes, and social drives.

Isi Igenegba is a Director at Strom Global Services, an indigenous oil and gas company she founded with her husband, with operations in Sub-Saharan Africa. They are blessed with two sons, Nathan and Judah.

In this season, Apostle Isi Igenegba stands as a prophetic voice, passionately heralding the call for transformation, revival, and Kingdom advancement. Her profound teachings, coupled with her infectious passion and love for people, inspire individuals to step out of their comfort zones, embrace their God-given purpose, and impact the world around them."

Made in the USA
Middletown, DE
26 November 2024

65474880R00123